ohn's Gospel called the "Spiritual Gospel"?
Vhat is the "messianic secret" in Saint
Mark? What is the status of the so-called
pocryphal gospels of Peter, Thomas, and
Matthias? Also of special interest are his
reatment of the synoptic problem, the au-
henticity and genuinity of Saint Luke's
Gospel, and the relationship of the Gospels
o each other.

The Four Gospels, however, is not in-
ended as a work of apologetics. It presents
hese Christian documents as they were
inderstood by the heirs of the apostolic
radition. The author stresses the importance
if purely critical and historical studies as
ntidotes of error, while he refutes advo-
ates of scepticism, vague mysticism, gnos-
icism, and schools of Protestant theology
hat belittle the historical value of the
Gospels and tend to existentialist interpreta-
ions. He challenges all those who stand
side and gaze at the so-called "ruins of the
Gospel" brought about, as they claim, by
cientific historical scholarship. He invites
ll to enter in and look at the Gospels as
hey were understood in their own times
y the people of the primitive Church.

THE AUTHOR

Monsignor Lucien Cerfaux, a Belgian
cholar and learned theologian, is at present
a Professor in the University of Louvain.
He holds a doctorate degree in Philosophy
nd Theology and has written extensively
on theological and scriptural topics.

Among his works translated into English
re: *Christ in the Theology of Saint Paul,
The Church in the Theology of Saint Paul,*
nd *Apostle and Apostolate.*

THE FOUR GOSPELS

An historical introduction
THE FOUR GOSPELS

The oral tradition;
Matthew, Mark, Luke and John;
the apocryphal gospels

Mgr L. Cerfaux
Professor in the University of Louvain

Translated by Patrick Hepburne-Scott
With an Introduction by
the Rev. Leonard Johnston L.S.S.

THE NEWMAN PRESS
WESTMINSTER, MD
DARTON, LONGMAN & TODD LTD
LONDON

DARTON, LONGMAN & TODD LTD
29A GLOUCESTER ROAD
LONDON SW7

THE NEWMAN PRESS
WESTMINSTER MD

Translated from *La Voix Vivante de l'Evangile au debut de l'Eglise* published by S.A. des Etablissements Casterman

This translation © *1960 Darton, Longman & Todd Ltd*
First Published 1960

Library of Congress Catalog Card No. 60-14818

PRINTED IN GREAT BRITAIN BY JARROLD AND SONS LTD., NORWICH; NIHIL OBSTAT ADRIANUS VAN VLIET, S.T.D., CENSOR DEPUTATUS. IMPRIMATUR E. MORROGH BERNARD, VIC. GEN., WESTMONASTERII, DIE 19A APRILIS, 1960. THE NIHIL OBSTAT AND IMPRIMATUR ARE A DECLARATION THAT A BOOK OR PAMPHLET IS CONSIDERED TO BE FREE FROM DOCTRINAL OR MORAL ERROR. IT IS NOT IMPLIED THAT THOSE WHO HAVE GRANTED THE NIHIL OBSTAT AND IMPRIMATUR AGREE WITH THE CONTENTS, OPINIONS OR STATEMENTS EXPRESSED.

102772

ANALYTICAL TABLE OF CONTENTS

vii

CHAPTER TWO. The Gospel according to Saint Matthew

CHAPTER FIVE. The Gospel of Saint John

CHAPTER SIX. The Tetramorphic Gospel

CHAPTER SEVEN. On the Fringes of the Four

CHAPTER EIGHT. Common Law under the Rule of the Crown

INTRODUCTION

'THE Word was made flesh. . . .' Our Lord is God made manifest in human form—historical, concrete, factual; he is 'that which our eyes have seen and our hands have handled of the word of life' (I John 1: 1).

And in the Gospel too the word becomes flesh—it is an historical, concrete, factual record of our Lord. And the two are intimately connected. It would have been of no value to us that the Word became flesh if after the few years of his mortal existence we lost contact with him; if all that were left to us were 'the Christ of faith'. There are people who claim that it was the faith of the Church which created the gospels; that the gospels are wonderful legends, pious imaginations in which the Church expressed its devotion to its leader. They then dismantle the solid edifice of the gospels in an attempt to get back to the Christ of history behind the Christ of faith. And when they find that their meddling brings down the building in ruins about their ears, they console themselves with the theory that it is after all faith alone which counts—like people who would have a roof over their heads with nothing to support it.

But the Christ of faith *is* the Christ of history. It is not the devotion of the Church which produced the gospels, but exactly the opposite—the gospels are the firm foundation of the Church's faith.

Christ is the Word of God; and the voice that enthralled the crowds on Galilean hills was conserved with passionate devotion by the apostles. And people hung upon the lips of the apostles because in their words they heard the Word of God. This was a living voice—the voice of Jesus re-echoed by the apostles. And when it was written down it did not become a dead letter; it was still living and life-giving. Here alone the Word of God was heard. And the Church fiercely defended this Word against attacks from all sides: from those who would add and from those who would take away; those who would add, like the apocryphal gospels with their colourful imaginations, or the Gnostics with their theory of secret information not contained in the gospels: and those who would take away, like the 'scholars' who would cut away the gospel story from the historical life of Christ in which it is rooted. The Church today holds the same faith as Irenaeus in the second century: 'We do not know the plan of our salvation in any other way than through the fourfold gospel.'

The fourfold gospel: for there is only one Gospel, one good news; but it has been expressed from four different points of view, the 'Gospel *according to* Matthew', and so on. These four different points of view are not an objection to the historical value of the Gospel; on the contrary, they are a testimony to it. It is precisely because the Good News is the news of God Himself, the Word of God, the fullness of truth, that it can be expressed in four quite different ways. We see this most clearly in the Fourth Gospel in which John, with an eagle's vision, surveys the life of our Lord from the heights of heaven. But it is equally true of each of the four, that each has his own way of presenting the truth. Very early in the history of the Church there was an attempt to combine all four gospels in one account; this was Tatian's *Diatessaron*, which had great popularity for a time. And since this time there have been sporadic attempts to do the same—to weave the four gospels into one so as not to miss any of the riches of any of them. But the Church has always come back to the four, realizing that even this work of piety was bound to take away something from the unique character of each.

We read each of the gospels in turn, then, knowing that in each of them the Word of God speaks to us in different accents. We retrace with loving care the process by which the living voice was recorded in faithful words. We seek to decipher the reasons which led the evangelists to record the news in precisely this form, the form proper to each of them. We strain our ears to hear every accent and shade of meaning in their words. This is a treasure of infinite value, to be contemplated infinitely. It is the Word of God, which is the food of our souls.

LEONARD JOHNSTON

TRANSLATOR'S NOTE

All New Testament texts in this book have been quoted from the Small Edition of *The Westminster Version of the Sacred Scriptures* (General Editors, Rev. Cuthbert Lattey, S.J. and Rev. John Murray, S.J.), Sands & Co. Ltd, London, 1947.

Quotations from ancient authors have been translated directly from Mgr Cerfaux's French version, after careful comparison with standard English translations. Among those consulted were the following:

Ancient Christian Writers (Longmans, Green and Co.), Volumes I and VI.

Library of Christian Classics (S.C.M. Press), Volumes I and II.

B. J. Kidd: *Documents illustrative of the History of the Church* (S.P.C.K.), Volume I.

H. Bettenson: *The Early Christian Fathers* (Oxford University Press).

H. Bettenson: *Documents of the Christian Church* (Oxford University Press).

M. R. James: *The Apocryphal New Testament* (Clarendon Press) corrected to 1953.

NOTE ON ANCIENT CHRISTIAN LITERATURE

St Clement of Rome, Pope (92–101)
Epistle to the Corinthians (about 96).

Epistle of Barnabas (96–98).

St Ignatius of Antioch (d. 107)
Letter to the Ephesians; — to the Magnesians; — to the Trallians; — to the Romans; — to the Philadelphians; — to the Smyrnaeans; and *— to Polycarp.*

St Polycarp (d. 156)
Letter to the Philippians.
The anonymous *Martyrium Polycarpi* (156–157).

St Papias, bishop of Hierapolis
Exposition of the Lord's Sayings (about 130).

Didache, or *Teaching of the Apostles* (probably about 150).

St Justin
First Apology (150–155).
Dialogue with Trypho the Jew (150–155).

Letter of the Christians of Lyons (177–178).

Basilides (130–140).

Valentinus (135–160).

Marcion (144–160).

Heracleon (145–180).

Tatian
Diatessaron (about 180).

St Irenaeus
Against the Heresies (about 180).

The Muratorian Canon (about 200).

St Hippolytus
  Philosophumena (after 222).

Tertullian (d. 222–223).

Clement of Alexandria (d. 211–215).

Origen (d. 244–255).

CHAPTER ONE

The 'Good News' and the Apostolic Tradition

THE starting-point of our Gospels is the actual life of our Lord and his teaching. This is that 'good news' which the Apostles preach. Preached by the Apostles, becoming the subject-matter of tradition and catechesis, the gospel material is gradually set in order to the point where it is collected in writings.

In this chapter we shall study the construction of the oral gospel, concluding with a word on present-day critical positions.

I

The Greek word transcribed by our word 'evangel' means, by etymology, the 'good news'. Like the corresponding verb 'evangelize', it is an ancient word, solemn and almost religious, of the Greek world. The herald brought the 'goods news' of victory, the city was beflagged and offered sacrifices to the gods who had saved them. The peaceful era of the Roman empire, and specially the birth of Augustus, were also 'good news'.

But we are in Palestine. What good news could be proclaimed there, if not that God had decided at last to intervene in favour of his people? The prophet Isaias had foretold that one day they would see on the mountains the feet of the heralds, publishing the great message. The day came when the voice of John the Baptist was heard in the wilderness proclaiming the good news: 'Prepare ye the way of the Lord! Do penance! The kingdom of heaven is at hand!' In the Baptist's mouth the 'good news' was couched in threatening terms. The Kingdom of God was being founded in judgment; fire from heaven had already come down on the earth; the axe is laid to the root of the tree.

Yet Galilee was shaken by a more violent disturbance. Jesus of Nazareth, who had received John's baptism, took up the sacred message: 'The kingdom of heaven is at hand! Do penance, and believe the good news!'

The threatening tones are soon submerged in joy. Jesus is surrounded by enthusiastic crowds. He speaks at length of the Kingdom. His hearers are skirting it, on its threshold; if they are willing to listen to the Master and to adopt the religious dispositions he suggests to them, they enter it, they are its subjects. The change of life required is a spiritual preparation. The poor, the meek, the gentle at heart, the pure, these are the native subjects of the Kingdom of God. The former 'justice' is replaced by a more perfect kind; the whole life of religion is deepened.

Jesus teaches. That is his way of founding the Kingdom of Heaven. To the disciples sent by John, impatient because he is so slow to inaugurate the judgment by fire from heaven, he replies: 'The blind see and the lame walk, lepers are cleansed and the deaf hear, and the dead rise and the poor receive the good news. Blessed is he that shall not be scandalized in me.'[1]

The word of Jesus, received in men's hearts, is the seed of the Kingdom; souls transformed by this word belong to the Kingdom and constitute it here on earth. The world is the field, souls are the crop which is ripening till the time of harvest. The Baptist thought only of gathering the crop into the barns, and (chiefly) of the fire which

---

[1] Mt. 11: 2–6

would consume the useless chaff. Jesus thinks of the sowing, the growing corn, the ripening grain.

The Kingdom on earth is founded on the teaching and also on the miracles of Jesus. The diseases and infirmities of men are the ransom-price of sin, they belong to the kingdom of evil. Jesus forces back the frontiers of this kingdom of evil, which has an unnatural life in diabolic possession. Jesus drives out devils. 'If by the Spirit of God I cast out devils, then is the kingdom of God come upon you.'

Jesus associates his Apostles with him in his work of recruiting for the Kingdom of God. They went round all the little towns of Galilee, announcing the good news.

According to exegetes of the 'eschatological'[2] school the good news preached by Jesus and his Apostles could only have been the end of the world and the setting up of the final, heavenly kingdom by a divine *coup d'état*. But the whole gospel tradition strikes another note, the note we have been trying to convey. Jesus and his Apostles did not solely, nor even principally, announce the end of the world. In the mind of Jesus, a spiritual kingdom was in course of being born here on earth. That was how the disciples understood it and saw it: the Kingdom was growing up in the footsteps of Jesus of Nazareth. That was the great hope which was arising and had even then begun to be realized. The good news was the presence of Jesus—the man they were to hail as the Messias at Caesarea Philippi; it was the new life he was bringing to birth, his teaching alive with divine power, his miracles.

From that moment the Christian 'evangel' has received its peculiar stamp. To begin with, the word will mean all

---

[2] Eschatology is the doctrine about the end of time. One school of exegesis has assumed the task of emphasizing the eschatology of the primitive Christian writings.

that has happened since the preaching of John: the arrival on the scene of Jesus the expected Messias, his teaching and his miracles. Later, it will include the story of his passion and his resurrection.

We know how things fell out. The word of Christ met with opposition. Under its guise of a message of joy, and because this joy was essentially spiritual, the teaching of Jesus was hard, it ran counter to accepted habits, to convenience, to the desire of immediate well-being and honours. The Pharisees and the Priests are hostile, the crowd falls away. The disciples of Jesus will now form a wandering community, already persecuted. This is already the Church in embryo and Jesus gives it its constitution. The earthly phase of the Kingdom of God begins in this way, like the mustard in its tiny seed.

Then the Messias' career was violently interrupted by his tragic death. To this day the narrative of the Passion bears the marks of the Apostles' confusion. But the Resurrection came.

2

After the Resurrection and the day of Pentecost the little messianic community regrouped itself around the Apostles and was soon swelled by new members. The Apostles were the witnesses of the Resurrection: they continued to preach the Kingdom of God and to found it, with redoubled and more enlightened enthusiasm.

The preaching of the good news begins to modify its content. Its emphasis will now be on the salvation offered to us by the death of Jesus and on the glory of his Resurrection. But it will also continue to stick closely to what it was at first, the shout of joy at the appearance of the Christ in Galilee, his message and his miracles.

The apostolic message will always contain these

elements: what Jesus taught, his miraculous deeds, his passion and his resurrection. When it solidifies into well-stocked narratives it will form what we now call 'the gospel'. That is what the word meant from the outset of the apostolic preaching: a life of Jesus, in short, but a life which saves us.

'The beginning of the Gospel of Jesus Christ'; so writes St Mark as the title of his book. 'The gospel', for this disciple of Peter, is the whole activity of Jesus of Nazareth. Matthew thinks the same. Recording Jesus' own words, he writes: 'Wheresoever this gospel is preached throughout the world, that which this woman had done shall be told for a memorial of her.'[3]

Luke, Paul's disciple, thinks no differently of the good news. In the prologue to the book of the Acts, when summing up his former book, which he certainly means to call a 'gospel', he tells us: 'The first account . . . told of all that Jesus began to do and to teach, until the day that he was taken up' (Acts 1: 1–2).

When it was necessary to choose a twelfth Apostle to take the place of Judas, the candidates had to fulfil two conditions: to be one of the disciples who had accompanied Jesus during all his earthly mission since the baptism of John and to have been a witness of the Resurrection (Acts 1: 21–22). The Resurrection is the object of the apostolic 'witness'; the mission of Jesus is the subject of the gospel.[4] The Apostle proclaims the whole of the good news and bears witness to the Resurrection.

Telling the life of Jesus and reproducing his teaching thus form integral parts of the apostolic message. How could it be otherwise? The Apostles had surely to continue their apostolic calling, just as Jesus had taught it to them.

[3] Mt. 26: 13   [4] See also Acts 2: 22; 10: 37–39; etc.

And how else could they do this but by repeating the message of the Kingdom, the teaching of Jesus, his miracles and his death, followed by his Resurrection?

Throughout history the gospel will never change its content.[5] It will always be 'the coming of the Saviour, our Lord Jesus Christ, his death and his Resurrection.'[6] 'As the Lord has taught in his "gospel",' says the *Teaching of the Apostles*, 'you will pray thus. . . .'[7]

The Jerusalem community was the first cradle of this gospel 'tradition', and by 'tradition' we mean here the manner, fixed by custom, of repeating the teachings, the events and the deeds of the life of Christ. In this community we find assembled all those who had been Jesus' friends: the Twelve, the 'brethren of the Lord', the holy women, the mother of Jesus and an important group of disciples. The community will grow, but it will always be centred closely round the Twelve, because they had seen and heard Jesus and had been chosen by him.

The Christian converts are first called 'disciples': disciples of Jesus, through the medium of the apostolic teaching.

'They persevered in the teaching of the Apostles.'[8] Now we know what that means. It was the doctrine and the works of Jesus which, through the Apostles' teaching, continued to attract these first 'Christians'. Years later we shall still meet with this passionate concern in the Christian conscience for the apostolic word, the voice which, in the words of Papias of Hierapolis (about 130), is 'living and permanent'.[9] The tradition which linked

[5] This is the agreed conclusion of the many recent works on the word 'Gospel'. Cf. R. Asting, *Die Verkündigung des Wortes im Urchristentum* (Stuttgart, 1939), pp. 445 ff.

[6] Ignatius, *ad Philad.* 9, 2

[7] *Did.* 8, 2, cf. 11, 3; 15, 3; cf. *Ep. Barn.* 5, 9; 8, 3

[8] Acts 2: 42   [9] Fragm. 11, 4

the life of the Church of his time directly with Christ was what mattered for Papias.

> If anyone turned up who had been in touch with the Elders, I used to enquire about their sayings, what Andrew or Peter had said, Philip or Thomas, James, John or Matthew or any other disciple of the Lord, and what Aristion and John the Elder now say, who are the Lord's disciples. In my opinion, books are not so useful as this living, permanent voice.[10]

At the end of the second century St Irenaeus, bishop of Lyons, says that he could still look back to the days of oral teaching, thanks to the lessons he had learnt from St Polycarp, the aged bishop of Smyrna:

> I can also tell . . . how he used to speak of his intercourse with John and the other disciples who had seen the Lord; how he recalled his sayings and the things he had heard them tell about the Lord, about his miracles as well as his teaching; how Polycarp had heard all this from eye-witnesses of the Word of Life and used to relate it in accordance with the Scriptures. By the mercy God has given us, I have listened carefully to these things too; I have guarded the memory of them, not on paper but in my heart. By God's grace I have always fondly meditated on them.[11]

Certain modern critics would have it that we are deceiving ourselves; they talk of the 'supreme indifference' to historical truth of the faith of these early Christians. These did not attempt to know or remember the sayings of Jesus; no, they invented them in the enthusiasm of faith or the outpourings of worship! We have just seen how opposed such an attitude is to that

[10] *Ibid.* Cf. G. Bardy, *La Théologie de l'Église, de saint Clément de Rome à saint Irénée* (Paris, 1945), p. 126

[11] *Epist. ad Florin.* (Eusebius, *H.E.*, V, 20, 6–7)

revealed by the primitive Christian documents. Should we hesitate to trust the men of those days, in a matter which touches them so nearly? The theory of these moderns is not in line with the facts; rather it shows that 'supreme indifference' to them of which they accuse the first Christians.

We appeal next to the style in which the reminiscences of Jesus, our Gospels, have come down to us. For those who know how to read them, these reminiscences bear the marks of a very primitive workmanship, enabling us to go back to the very earliest days of the Church. Let us look first at Christ's discourses to the crowd, and especially the Sermon on the Mount, a typical discourse. We can recognize in it a very marked kind of style: 'It is certain', writes Loisy, 'that the discourses in the Gospels, even those in the fourth, were originally short writings composed in the rhythmic form peculiar to the poetic writings of the Old Testament (Psalms, Proverbs, and the discourses in Job).'[12] Under the intentional or unintentional confusions of this remark, the admission is worth remembering.

The discourses in the first three Gospels show marked resemblances to the rhythmic passages of the Old Testament. To be precise, it is not in the didactic books or the Psalms that we must look for the closest analogies, but in the Prophets. The gospel discourses have the same kind of rhythm as the prophecies of Isaias and Amos, just because they were both delivered publicly, in a style suitable for such solemn discourses, addressed to the crowds. This style has been very aptly called the 'oral style'.[13] We come across it in the most various surround-

[12] *The Birth of the Christian Religion*, tr. L. P. Jacks, London, 1948, p. 43
[13] M. Jousse, 'Le Style Oral et Mnémotechnique chez les Verbomoteurs' (*Archives de Philosophie*, vol. II, cah. 4; Paris, 1925)

ings, wherever the habit of writing has not abolished the more instinctive form of the spoken tongue. It seems that similar elements can always be discerned in it, the balancing of rhythm, mnemonic techniques, repetitions, alliterations and rhymes, besides literary forms, comparisons, images, etc., forming a sort of verbal treasury on which the composer's memory can always draw.

We find these elements in every case among the prophets, as in the gospel discourses; in spite of some centuries separating them—but literary recipes are long-lived—we are in the same Palestinian setting. The 'oral style' is alive there, or surviving.

Isaias spoke in this style. His prophecies, before being written down, were delivered in public. We nearly always possess the actual words of these compositions, arranged with consummate art. Their rhythm will not survive translation: but we can get an idea of it by strongly accenting the chief words (usually three) forming the framework of the phrase:

> The *ox knoweth* his *owner*
> and the *ass* his *master's crib*;
> but *Israel* doth *not know*,
> my *people* doth *not consider*.[14]

Isaias is a great artist, a genius of the spoken word. So is Jesus in his own way, which is freer, less tied to his system. We might place the gospel manner somewhere between that of Isaias and that of Amos, which is much less brilliant and polished. Any religious orator, borne along by the religious influence of the prophets, would have employed this style. Jesus handled it with sovereign authority.

The 'oral style' was made to impress the masses and

[14] Is. 1: 3

take root in their memory, for the genius of the 'reciters' of this style was matched by the talent of the 'repeaters', accustomed by the very necessities of the case to remember these rhythmic compositions by heart. This style explains how it was possible to preserve, without writing, the spoken addresses of Jesus, and how we possess them in their primitive terms, in all the freshness and vivacity they took from the Master's word. If the Gospel of St Matthew has preserved the oral style of the discourses more carefully than the others, may it not be because the tax-collector of Capharnaum possessed the talent of a 'reciter'? It would have been the only earthly gift he did not give up. Here is an example of these 'recitatives':

> Lay not up for yourselves treasures on earth,
>   where moth and rust consume,
>   and where thieves break in and steal;
> But lay up for yourselves treasures in heaven,
>   where neither moth nor rust consume,
>   and where thieves break not in nor steal.
> For where thy treasure is,
>   there will thy heart be also.[15]

Discourses thus composed have all the elegance and style needed to become 'tradition'. The community repeated them after the Apostles; they constituted the treasure on which the 'Scribes of the Kingdom of Heaven' could draw.

Others of Jesus' discourses were intimate instructions to his disciples. The Palestinian world was accustomed to oral teaching and quite content to be nourished by it. The Doctors of the Law did not write at all; their disciples learned by heart their masters' opinions, which passed on in the same form from mouth to mouth. This is, in fact,

[15] Mt. 6: 19–21

just what 'tradition' is by definition; the master 'hands over' to his disciple (almost like a secret, like an initiation to his thought) his own doctrine and that which he has received from his masters. The gospel 'tradition' is modelled on these customs. The same Palestinian setting explains too the presence in the Gospels of numerous 'controversies' between Jesus and the Pharisees or the Sadducees. Finding themselves exposed to the same attacks that Jesus had met, the disciples memorized his typical, scathing replies, placing them very briefly in some schematized context.

The Gospel narratives too received their distinctive stamp in the primitive community, to become the subject-matter of tradition. Consider, for instance, those stories of miracles, very short, stripped down, reduced to their essential points. The actual reality must have been complicated, as it always is; the story has 'set' into its simplest version, simple but vivid, and expressive because of its very brevity.

A leper drew near and worshipped him, saying, 'Lord, if thou wilt, thou canst make me clean.' And stretching forth his hand he touched him, saying, 'I will; be thou made clean.' And straightway his leprosy was cleansed. And Jesus saith to him, 'See thou tell no man, but go, show thyself to the priest. . . .'[16]

The calls of the first disciples (Mt. 4: 18–22) are in the same key. Only the salient features and words are preserved, all the stronger for their isolation.

Such, in substance, is our gospel material: material of a community 'tradition', easy to remember, reduced to its bare essentials; exactly what it had to be if it were to be established and survive in the community at Jerusalem,

[16] Mt. 8: 2–4

united under the Apostles, the witnesses and intermediaries between Jesus and the disciples of those first days.[17]

The very language of our Gospels proves the Palestinian origin of the tradition. This argument needs prudent handling. It is obviously not enough to show that vocabulary and style are Aramaic in background. Except for St Luke, the evangelists spoke Aramaic as their mother-tongue. Their Greek was rather a dialect, a Greek debased by Aramaic. But the evangelists' style reveals something else. Under a surface of Greek which may be of very good quality, the fundamental expressions of their thought are reflections of Aramaic. Such formulas, for instance, as 'Kingdom of the heavens', 'Son of Man', 'do his justice', etc., can only be rightly understood when retranslated. They introduce us to a milieu which is not the Greek world but the Palestinian: always their flavour is that of the Old Testament and later Judaism. The more complex arrangements of these expressions, besides, are not those of the Greek language. The phrase is articulated otherwise than in Greek, the order of the words is that of the Aramaic statement. When the Gospels construct a longer phrase, it is not in order to display the supple ordering of the Greek sentence, but to develop strophes, as it were, formed of sentences in juxtaposition, balancing each other parallelwise. Compositions of this sort must not only have been written by Semites; they must have originated and survived in the Palestinian setting which was that of Jesus and his first disciples. Being simple transpositions from the Aramaic, they are excellent guarantees of the honesty of the gospel memoirs.

The transcription of the Aramaic memoirs into Greek was made at Jerusalem itself, in the presence of the Apostles, in the earliest days of the Christian Church.

[17] Cf. Th. Soiron, *Die Logia Jesu* (Münster, 1916)

From the beginning the Church had gained converts among the 'Hellenistic' Jews of Jerusalem. Whereas the Galilean Apostles (with the exception of St Matthew, and perhaps of St Philip and the sons of Zebedee) could hardly understand Greek, and Aramaic was in any case their mother-tongue, the Hellenists talked Greek among themselves and received an education of the Greek type. They were in fact Jews born among the Dispersion, at Alexandria, Cyrene, Cilicia or Rome. The cases of Philo —an outstanding achievement—of Apollos, a convert from Alexandria, of St Paul, of Barnabas and of Stephen, all give us some idea of the Jews' ability to assimilate the culture as well as the language of Greece.

The incident of the choice of the seven deacons— all Hellenistic Jews—shows us the importance of the Hellenistic element in the Jerusalem church. That the Hellenistic section of the community was concerned from the outset about the preservation of the Christian memoirs and therefore contributed to recording them in Greek, is vividly indicated in a document used by St Luke in the Acts, a description of the Jerusalem community drawn up directly in Greek, with some claim to literary merit. The same Hellenists must have taken an active part in the formation of a Greek gospel tradition, reproducing the Aramaic. It was in this bilingual society in Jerusalem that our tradition, still preserving its fundamentally Aramaic flavour, fixed its Greek vocabulary and pre-pared to conquer the Graeco-Roman world. G. Dalman, one of the greatest experts on the Aramaic-speaking world, stresses this bilingualism which facilitated the first attempts at the change-over to Greek. He writes:

That Jesus and his circle understood several languages, and that this was also true of the first community (Acts 6: 1), is a historical fact of some importance. It follows that even the original form of Jesus' words, which still underlies our Gospels, came into existence among people who shared with Jesus and his first disciples their know- ledge of the world-wide language. That is a guarantee that our Gospels, in all essentials, will be a faithful trans- lation of the original thoughts of Jesus. There is no need to guess at the tenor of their original, for in the Greek text we have a firm bridge by which we can reach it. But that does not excuse us from the duty of crossing the bridge, a bridge stretching between two worlds which, in spite of all their resemblances, are widely estranged from each other, the world of Plato and Phidias on one side, that of Moses and the Jewish scribes on the other.[18]

It is in fact by no means unimportant that the bridge between the Aramaic gospel tradition and its Greek counterpart was built in Jerusalem, in the apostolic com- munity. It has been suggested that the Greek tradition originated at Antioch in Syria, which after Jerusalem was the second centre of Christianity. The thesis that the church of Antioch was of decisive importance in the formation of Christian doctrine was advanced by Bousset in a famous book,[19] and has since been often repeated. It is at the root of many of the assertions of that school of criticism which regards our Gospels as the creations of theology and worship.

It is therefore not rash to admit [wrote Loisy] that it was in this second home of the Gospel (Antioch), in this first home of Hellenistic Christianity, that the Christian religion was really outlined. It was there, in the first place, that the gatherings definitely assumed the character of a cult and a worship of the Lord Jesus; it was there that Jesus became most specially the Lord; it was there that Baptism became a consecration and initiation to this

[18] *Jesus-Jeschua* (Leipzig, 1922), p. 6
[19] *Kyrios Christos* (1st ed., Göttingen, 1913)

cult of the Lord Christ; there that the Eucharistic Supper, instead of being wholly taken up with his memory and a kind of foretaste of his coming again, was conceived in the manner of the sacrificial meals, as an act of present communion with his sublime personality. . . . The atmosphere of this mysticism is no longer that of the Gospel; as far as we can judge, it was not even that of the messianic mysticism of the first community.[20]

From these premisses the conclusion will be drawn that our Gospels form the manuals of the mystic cult of the Lord Jesus.

Yet a valid history of Christianity, history that can provide an interpretation of the documents, goes counter to this view which rends the primitive Church in two and treats the churches in pagan lands as a formation independent of Jerusalem. Barnabas, the Apostles' envoy, 'inspected' the church of Antioch. The Galilean Apostles, and not least Peter, were fully at home in the Gentile churches; Antioch, presumably Corinth, and certainly Rome, all saw Peter. At Corinth a faction in the church called itself the party of Cephas. In the Pauline churches themselves it was regretted that St Paul had not known Jesus. As for St Paul, he was too great a man to think that he could cut the painter. These are facts, of infinitely greater weight than the hypotheses referred to, simply making them unnecessary. The problem of the birth of the Greek gospel tradition had been solved before the foundation of the church of Antioch and the Pauline churches. Details could still be adapted, but by and large the gospel material we possess goes back to the apostolic Church.

St Paul is an apostle apart from the others. His education, his history, his strong personality and the mission he received from God all prevent him from speaking exactly like the others. In his mouth the word 'gospel' takes on a new significance, in conformity with the Christian message as he understands it. For Paul had not been a witness of Christ's life. He had been given the grace of an appearance of the risen Christ, who had converted him to Christianity by revealing to him the Christian salvation. It is this salvation through the death and resurrection of Christ, which he preaches to the pagan world. It is this message of salvation which he calls 'the gospel'. But on this point St Paul founded no school. The name of 'gospel' continued to be applied to the Good News as it had been preached by the Twelve, including the life of Jesus as well as his death and his resurrection.

All this is only a question of vocabulary. Fundamentally St Paul agrees with the Twelve. He says once in passing that it is useless to have known 'Christ according to the flesh',[21] in the sense of Christ lacking the power of spiritual renewal which comes from his death and his resurrection. But this is an over-statement, a theological affirmation insufficiently qualified. All Christianity's love for the teaching and example of Christ belies him and Paul belies himself. In fact he is the first to appeal to the Lord's commands and examples and to the traditions of the Jerusalem church which come directly from the Master. He knows that the virtues he preaches, the form of the Christian life, humility, charity and chastity, have Christ as their lawgiver. All these convictions, which are now his life, his joy and his very mind, had been given to him by Christ, who had revealed them to the Apostles even before sending them the Holy Spirit who was to complete their formation.

[21] 2 Cor. 5: 16

In the course of his Christian career, before embarking on his conquests, Paul had been in contact with Peter, John and James, the Lord's 'brother'. He had worked with Barnabas' team in the church at Antioch; the traditions of this church recorded that he had been a prophet, but also a *didaskalos*, that is, one who had taught the doctrine of Jesus.[22] He continued to train his Christians by teaching them to imitate Jesus and obey his commandments.

We understand Paul very ill if we make him a man purely 'spiritual', supremely indifferent to those teachings of Christ which the primitive Church lovingly learned from the lips of the Galilean Apostles. To contrast him with the Galilean Apostles, as if they alone had remained faithful to the teaching of Christ, is to distort the whole history of primitive Christianity.

Fidelity to the historical memoirs of the life of Christ and to his teaching is an essential element of the Christianity of the Apostles, of Paul, of the apostolic Fathers and of the whole Catholic Church, which is but the continuation of the primitive Church. There is only one Christianity, because fidelity to Christ has never varied. So far from diminishing respect for the traditions, religious feeling only strengthens it. Such at least is the view which emerges from all our documents. A community which deliberately built up the life of Christ, with the needs of its theology and worship in view, is a pure myth, typical of all those which our self-styled scientific age too often succeeds in inventing and imposing.

3

Analysis of the gospel material shows us how certain conglomerations of primitive memoirs were formed, for

[22] Acts 13: 1

tradition is not preserved as a nebula of particles with no cohesion. From the beginning it is grouped around certain centres of interest which are fairly easy to discover. Concerning Christ's teachings the principal centres of interest are seen in three long discourses: the Sermon on the Mount, the parables and the missionary charge.

The lion's share falls to the Sermon on the Mount, which provides us with a summary of Christ's teaching, a primitive catechism. It is, we may say, the type-sermon. Its existing version in St Matthew's Gospel is no doubt artificial. All the same, the Sermon on the Mount is a good representative of the type of sermon Jesus delivered in Galilee. That is not all, for the main themes of his teaching, themes which did not vary much at bottom and could be adapted to different audiences according to circumstances, are well represented in this queen of sermons, a sort of classic of the Master's teaching.

The parable discourses correspond to another type of instructions. Men were struck by this very particular type of teaching; they recalled them and made collections of them. Two or three chief groups are evident: the 'parables of the Kingdom' in Matthew 13, the eschatological parables which point to the end of time, and the parables on the Christian virtues, preserved for us by St Luke.

The first Christian missionaries needed a 'highway code': so the charges given by our Lord when he sent out his Apostles in Galilee and later the Seventy-two disciples, and when he foretold future missions, were put together. All these sayings, uttered in different circumstances, make up the missionary charge.

To these first discourses, which are fundamental in the constitution of the apostolic memoirs, were later added an 'ecclesiastical' discourse (counsels given by our Lord to his disciples when they were with him in the desert, forming an embryo community, the discourse condemning the Pharisees and the eschatological discourse.

The elements of tradition could be grouped according to typical subjects; description of a journey (the circuit round the lake), recollections of the mutual relations of two teachers (those of Jesus and the Baptist), or a teacher's day (the day at Capharnaum). The mission of John, the baptism of Jesus and the temptation in the desert form a sort of 'overture' to the gospel story. An entire section was formed round the multiplication of the loaves and another round the Transfiguration.

The incidents of the Passion very soon became a consecutive story, to which the secondary actors of the drama contributed: the Twelve, Peter, John, the holy women. On the occasion of the celebration of the Eucharistic Supper, 'the eve of the day in which he was betrayed', they recalled the memories of it and arranged them whilst re-enacting them. The biographical character of this section is very marked, as it is with the story of the last journey by Jericho to Jerusalem, which forms a sort of preface to the Passion narrative. The series of appearances of the risen Christ form other very characteristic groups.

With all this we find ourselves on mixed ground, between purely oral tradition and the first written schemes. In all probability these were more numerous than we imagine. Numerous were the *didaskaloi* who used memoranda-books; St Luke tells us of many attempts at systematization which he had been able to consult.[23] The very complex and tangled state in which the tradition reaches us, when we make contact with it

[23] Lk. 1: 1

in our present Gospels, also suggests that there must have been a pre-history, most probably not of purely oral tradition, preceding the final stage in which the memoirs were fixed in the canonical Gospels.

The first arrangement of the partial syntheses to which we have alluded, one which was impressed on all subsequent literary tradition, may be reconstructed as follows.

There exist two main series of sources, each homogeneous in itself and partly contrasted with the other. The first series covers the activity of Jesus in Galilee and continues with the teachings to the community in the desert and the controversies, the condemnation of the Pharisees and the eschatological discourse. All this series is, we may say, of Galilean inspiration. It represents the memories preserved by the Twelve about the teachings of the Master and the miraculous works of Christ, revealing himself as founder of the Kingdom and Son of God; we could call it the story of the teachings and miracles of Christ.

The story of the Passion is the central core of a consecutive narrative which begins with the first warning of the Passion at Caesarea Philippi. The death of Christ, followed by the Resurrection, constitutes a new centre of interest, quite different from that which governed the composition of the first series. Jesus is no longer the herald of the good news; he is the subject of it, the good news being the news of salvation won by his death and resurrection.

The plan of our Gospels shows how these two first narrative syntheses were amalgamated, welded together by the section on the loaves. It begins with the Galilean ministry, drawn from the 'teaching and miracles' source. Next it combines with the Passion source the material which (perhaps in a later edition) completed the 'teaching

and miracles' source, that is, the teaching in the desert
and the final condemnation of the Pharisees and of
Judaism. To conclude the gospel, the appearance of Jesus
on the mountain in Galilee was related, with the sending
of the Twelve to the Gentiles. This last episode is conceived in the spirit of the 'teaching and miracles' source
and gives unity to the whole: the Resurrection gives the
disciples their official investiture with the Spirit and with
the Christ, now Son of God in power; clothed with power
from on high, they will go out to repeat to the nations
what Christ taught in Galilee.

4

The point of view we have outlined in the preceding
pages is amply supported by our documents, and is also
inspired by the most recent criticism. We would approve
the latter unreservedly, were it not for its unjustified
mistrust of tradition. Let us remind ourselves of its stages.

It began by exaggerating the very real eschatological
aspect of our Lord's teaching. The good news which he
proclaimed (and we are assured he cannot have preached
for more than a few months) only looked to the last
judgment: the Apostles must have taken up the same
message. Loisy writes:

> The imminent return of Christ Jesus to the earth had
> been proclaimed for many years before the story was told,
> in oral preaching and in evangelical writings, of what in
> detail Jesus had done, taught and suffered before ascend-
> ing into heaven to prepare the day of God. The Gospel
> was the announcement of this coming Day before it
> became an account of the Christ's teaching and of his
> saving death.[24]

[24] *The Birth of the Christian Religion*, p. 33

On the contrary, we see that our Lord founded the Kingdom on earth. The 'good news' was *the Kingdom*, as much in its earthly phase as in its final, eschatological phase. The Apostles told how the Kingdom was founded by the teaching, the miracles and the death and resurrection of Christ: that is the Christian 'good news', the Gospel.

The eschatological school is now better informed. It often admits that the 'Kingdom of God' was simply the natural form in which Christ's religious thought was clothed, and that it expresses an actual religion and a morality of abiding value. We agree, provided they are really willing to admit that Jesus also founded, here on earth, a messianic community which was the Church.

The attention of the critics was next directed to the formation of the gospel tradition, and the factors which governed it. It was certainly a forward step in exegesis to determine more exactly the 'literary forms' in which the tradition flowed.[25] We have spoken of 'controversies', of 'stories', of the call of the Apostles, of 'miracles'. . . . We are perfectly willing to add apophthegms (pithy aphorisms, often introduced by a short story), maxims, proverbial 'sayings', legislative regulations. There is nothing to stop us treading in the critics' footsteps, provided it be granted that the actual sayings, the actual facts, take shape quite normally, without distortion, in the already existing literary forms. The 'News from all Quarters' column in a newspaper is a literary form too, and obeys certain laws: the local correspondents, when they report a fire, resort to clichés. Does it follow there was never any fire? We crave pardon for such a *simpliste* argument, but it is neither more nor less so than

[25] The fundamental book is that of R. Bultmann, *Die Geschichte der Synoptischen Tradition* (1st ed., Göttingen, 1921; 2nd ed., 1931)

the fundamental fallacy of the school which calls itself 'the method of the history of literary forms', and denies in principle the objective truth of every story whose 'form' already existed.

Then the attempt was made to determine the various factors which governed this supposedly creative evolution of the gospel tradition. It was reduced to two principles, theology and worship. In conjunction, they are supposed to have transformed the figure of Jesus in accordance with the desires, needs and dreams of an enthusiastic community. Loisy sententiously declares: 'The Gospels when closely examined are far less the echoes of a tradition zealous to keep intact the memories of Jesus, than a didactic instrument, we might even say, a catechism of the worship rendered to the Lord Jesus.'[26]

And so by dint of seeking the interests of the community in the transformation of the figure of Jesus—from the 'eschatological' prophet to the God above all the gods of paganism—they came to forget the essential factor of tradition, or to put it in the shade. O. Cullmann, for example, wrote: 'For we know that every single paragraph was passed by the community before being fixed in writing, and was therefore subjected to the influence of a great many factors. Now, among these there is not found precisely that factor in which the authenticity of a story consists: the concern for history.'[27]

Obviously all depends on the sense of the word 'history'. Admittedly, it was not the love of science which inspired these first believers, it was the love of Christ. But this love is itself a pledge of fidelity. The earliest

[26] *The Birth of the Christian Religion*, p. 43
[27] 'Les Récentes Etudes sur la Formation de la Tradition Evangélique', in *Revue d'Histoire et de Philosophie Religieuses*, 1925, p. 472. In contrast to this, Cullmann's later works show his respect for the gospel tradition.

Christian community, inspired by this love, wished to keep faithful to the teaching and the example of the Master as the Apostles bore witness to it. This witness, 'the living and permanent voice', is the source of our Gospels.

CHAPTER TWO

The Gospel According to Saint Matthew

I n the second century, when our four Gospels were copied into one volume (probably by this time a 'codex'),[1] they were distinguished from each other by the formula: 'according to Matthew', 'according to Mark', etc. It was the one and only Gospel, the 'good news' of the message, presented by Matthew or the other evangelists.

In point of fact, Matthew's Gospel is not quite like the others. It might very well be called 'the Gospel' *par excellence.* In this Gospel, all the streams of tradition are canalized in writing; it sets down what all the Apostles preached about Jesus. Matthew gave it his name, not because he was its 'author', as we now understand the term, but because he was the 'servant' of the common tradition to the extent of becoming its first secretary. It was he who, as Papias put it, 'composed' or set in order the primitive memoirs. Was it not rather in the line of his profession as tax-collector to take notes and classify? He is hardly more than a secretary: his person is sunk in his work. His work, then, is our subject.

I

All the records preserved by the Christian communities about the writing of our Gospels give Matthew the first

[1] The 'codex' is in the shape of a modern book, made up of 'quires' sewn together. The 'codex' is distinguished from the 'roll' of papyrus or parchment. Its name describes its appearance: it is a long strip rolled on itself.

place, and date its composition in that primitive period when the discourses of Jesus and the events of his life were still current in their Aramaic dress.

'Matthew set in order the Lord's teachings [*ta logia*] in Aramaic: everyone translated them as best he could.'[2] These are the words of Papias, in the year A.D. 130, that bishop of Hierapolis we have already mentioned, whom Irenaeus calls 'a fine old man, a hearer of John (the Apostle) and the companion of Polycarp'.[3]

St Irenaeus states the same fact with more precision: 'Matthew both preached the gospel and set it in writing among the Palestinians, in their own language, while Peter and Paul were preaching in Rome and founding the Roman church.'[4] For Irenaeus, as appears from the context, Matthew's Gospel is the earliest in date, and Papias does not disagree. This is then the tradition of the Asiatic Christians, backed by the authority of John the Apostle.

Eusebius of Caesarea, our first historian of the Church, reports an ancient tradition according to which Pantaenus, founder of that catechetical school of Alexandria later to be adorned by Clement and Origen, went to India and among the Christians of that country found a copy of the Gospel of Matthew in Aramaic writing, which these people said they had received from the Apostle Bartholomew.[5]

The Christian literature of the age of the apostolic Fathers (St Clement of Rome's Epistle to the Corinthians, the *Teaching of the Apostles*, the Letters of St Ignatius of Antioch and St Polycarp, the Epistle of pseudo-Barnabas,

[2] Papias, *Fragm.* II, 16
[3] Eusebius, *H.E.*, III, 39, 1; cf. Iren. *Adv. Haer.*, V, 33, 4
[4] Irenaeus, *Adv. Haer.*, III, 1, 1; Eusebius, *H.E.*, V, 8, 2
[5] *H.E.*, V, 10

Valentinus) makes almost exclusive use of Matthew's Gospel, which impregnates it with the teachings of Christ.[6] So we are true to the mind of the first generations of Christians when we represent the Gospel of St Matthew as 'the Gospel' *par excellence*.

True, a thorny question arises, for we no longer possess the Aramaic Gospel; in its place we read a Gospel in Greek. But our position is exactly the same as that of all the ancients whose evidence we have just quoted. When they described as they did the Aramaic Gospel, which they distinguished from the Greek Gospel, they perfectly understood that they were taking the same attitude to the canonical Greek Gospel, for they regarded it as the equivalent of the primitive Gospel.

But we must not treat these points without regard to our ancestors' literary customs. They never had our anxiety for minute exactness. It was enough for them if a translation—an interpretation, as they would say—preserved all the wealth of the original. It mattered little if it added a style of its own to the work it transcribed. This was the case, for example, with the Septuagint version of the Hebrew scriptures.

This remark applies in the present case. Some have claimed to prove that our Greek Gospel of Matthew is inspired by the Gospel of Mark, particularly in the order of certain episodes and also in the style of the narratives. It is possible. The inter-relations of our first three Gospels, especially of Matthew and Mark, pose an extremely complicated question, for which no *simpliste* solution exists. Any simple solution stands condemned in advance. The physical and mathematical sciences try to reduce phenomena to unity, but this method cannot be forcibly

[6] This is well brought out in E. Massaux, *Influence de l'Évangile de saint Matthieu sur la Littérature Chrétienne avant saint Irénée* (Louvain, 1950)

imposed on us in history, where any hypothesis must take account of the complexity of the facts.

There is nothing to prevent us admitting both of these two propositions: first, that the Gospel of Matthew in its Aramaic form was the first of them all; secondly, that the same Gospel, in its Greek form, has borrowed something from St Mark.

As against a certain number of critics, but in accordance with the data of tradition, we presume Matthew's Aramaic work to have been a genuine Gospel, not a mere conglomeration of the Lord's discourses. Analysis of the synoptic Gospels, as well as probability, seems to justify the tradition. Once men wanted to set down the riches of the gospel in writing they could not confine themselves to discourses. These would have to be framed in a story which explained them and gave their setting. If we study closely the matter and the arrangement of the first Greek Gospel it will be apparent that it is richer than Mark's Gospel, even as to the narratives, and that its view of the life of Christ simply cannot be explained as starting from Mark; it is independent of it. On the other hand, one is led to the conjecture that Luke knew, besides Mark's Gospel, a gospel story which resembles Matthew.[7] These two sets of considerations combine to make us admit that the formation of the Greek Matthew and of Luke was influenced by a primitive gospel, which it seems right to identify (as does all tradition) with the Aramaic Matthew. We believe we should go further and say that the primitive gospel of Matthew was known to Mark and that the cause of the *basic* resemblance between the first two Gospels is not that our Greek Matthew drew its gospel

---

[7] L. Cerfaux, 'A propos des Sources du Troisième Évangile: Proto-Luc óu Proto-Matthieu', in *Ephemérides theol. lovanienses*, t. XII (1935), pp. 5–27, or in *Recueil L. Cerfaux*, I, pp. 389–414

material from Mark but that the Aramaic Matthew has for ever stamped the narrative with the imprint given it by Matthew, the secretary of the primitive tradition.

2

We are then justified in treating Matthew, even our Greek Matthew, as the original Gospel, at least as regards the public life and the Passion. The reader can guess the reason for this last qualification. The gospel means first and foremost the public life and its tragic consummation. When the infancy-gospel came to be added to the primitive core, a biographical interest was introduced which modified the earlier conception of the gospel as *message*. In this respect our Greek Matthew is in advance of Mark, which remains more faithful to the primitive conception, more archaic and conservative.

We can quite easily detect, still showing through our Gospel, the primitive arrangement of gospel memoirs which we have already outlined,[8] combining two main series of sources: the story of Christ's teaching and miracles and the story of his Passion, beginning with the events at Caesarea Philippi.

The first narrative (the life of the Teacher of doctrine) is built up on five great discourses: the Sermon on the Mount, the missionary charge, the parables, the discourse to the disciples, and finally, forming a single piece, the condemnation of the Pharisees and the eschatological discourse. These discourses mark five stages and show us the system both of the Saviour's teaching and of all his activity. A period of success, very marked in the two first discourses, is ended by a crisis which isolates Jesus from the Jewish people. The Pharisees are hostile, the crowd holds more and more aloof. The parables are the actual

[8] See Chap. 1, sec. 3, p. 20)

form of teaching which mark the crisis; according to whether men agree to understand them or refuse to attend to them, they are on Jesus' side or against him. Henceforth Jesus will speak for the benefit of his disciples and legislate for the little community that is still faithful to him; on the other hand, he will bring unbelief to a head by denouncing the Pharisees and proclaiming, together with the end of the world, the final chastisement of the nation which has rejected him.

That this first narrative was built up on the discourses is still clear in the present text. Before two of the chief discourses, the Sermon on the Mount and the parables discourse, the scene is solemnly set. We are shown Christ's two pulpits: the mountain where, surrounded by his Apostles, he speaks to the crowd seated at his feet, and the boat on the lake of Capharnaum, where he addresses the crowd, massed in a circle round him on the banks. After each of the discourses appears the stereotyped formula: 'And it came to pass, when Jesus had brought these words to a close . . .'[9] After the last discourse the formula is given an extra word: '. . . brought *all* these words to a close'.

Without being in any way 'padding', the remainder of the narrative is subordinate to the discourses, either introducing them or noting their effects. It has been suggested that this division into five great discourses may be connected with the title of the work by Papias: 'The five volumes [*tomes*] of the expositions of the Lord's teachings.' We would not insist on this, but we shall use this expression 'volume', which is convenient, in our analysis.

The second narrative, beginning with Jesus' withdrawal to the desert, overlaps with the first to begin with,

[9] 7: 28; 11: 1; 13: 53; 19: 1; 26: 1

because its beginning covers the same period as the two final stages of the career of Christ as teacher. But it is sharply distinguished from the first narrative; its centre of interest is now the approach of Christ's Passion and Resurrection, rather than his teaching. With this narrative, which leads to the Passion at Jerusalem, we connect the withdrawal to the desert with the two multiplications of the loaves, next the events grouped around Caesarea Philippi, and then the ascent to Jerusalem.

On these lines we would suggest the following scheme for St Matthew's Gospel. Five volumes present the story of the teaching of Jesus, first in Galilee (the three first volumes), then in the desert (volume IV) and in Jerusalem (volume V). From this first gospel theme we distinguish a second, that of the Passion, which we take to start with the section about the multiplications of the loaves. Italics are used to distinguish this second gospel narrative.

PROLOGUE or infancy-gospel (1–2).

FIRST PART: The teaching in Galilee.

Vol. I.   (1) Beginning of ministry: two 'trilogies' (3–4).
           (2) Sermon on the Mount (5–7).
           (3) A journey (8–9: 34).
Vol. II.   (1) Preamble to missionary charge (9: 35–10: 4).
           (2) Missionary charge (10: 5–42).
Vol. III. (1) Opposition and contradiction (11: 1–12: 50).
           (2) The Parables (13: 1–52).
           (3) Jesus despised in his own country (13: 53–58).

SECOND PART: The Master an outlaw.

Section on the multiplications of the loaves
(14: 1–16: 12).
After Caesarea Philippi; the Transfiguration
(16: 13–17: 13).
Vol. IV. (1) Introduction (17: 14–27).
   (2) Ecclesiastical discourse (18).
   (3) Episodes in Judaea (19: 1–20: 16).
Ascent to Jerusalem, and first encounters
(20: 17–22: 14).
Vol. V. (1) Controversies (22: 15–46).
   (2) Discourse against the Pharisees (23).
   (3) Eschatological discourse (24–25).

THIRD PART: The consummation.

The Passion (26–27).
The Resurrection (28).

We can and indeed should consider Matthew's work in one comprehensive view, for he intelligently amalgamates the two primitive gospel narratives. Let us complete its analysis, looking at it as a well-planned literary construction.

The first volume opens with two trilogies. The first consists of the mission of the Baptist, the baptism of Jesus and the temptation in the desert: that is the traditional overture to the 'gospel'. The second 'sites' the mission of Jesus (in Galilee and Capharnaum) and tells of the first calls and the first successes. We are thus made ready to listen to the Sermon on the Mount. Jesus is received in the synagogues: he announces the 'gospel of the Kingdom', relying on the people's passionate expectation and endeavouring to transform it. The Reign of God begins: diseases are banished, devils are put to flight and a huge crowd follows the conquering Messias.

After the Sermon on the Mount, St Matthew, having

given us a type-discourse, now gives us a type-journey, a missionary journey in the neighbourhood of Caphar-naum, centre of the Saviour's activity. He emphasizes Jesus' miraculous power over sickness and death, over the devils and the tempestuous sea. New disciples are called and already there are signs of the conflict between Jesus and the Pharisees.

A preamble was needed in order to give the setting of the missionary discourse to the Twelve, so a summary sketch is given of Jesus' work in Galilee and the distress of souls waiting for the Kingdom: twelve disciples are to be chosen to extend the mission.

After the mission of the Twelve the movement of opposition to Jesus begins to sharpen. In contrast with the corresponding section of Mark, this is one of the sections which best shows the wealth of information in the first Gospel as well as its penetrating psychology. The evangelist has grasped the component elements of the drama of Jesus' career, and here he brings together in a vivid combination all the misunderstandings which were to precipitate the end. It is a sort of fresh start to the gospel story, now placed under the sign of failure and contradiction. The Baptist aptly reappears to open this second act of the Gospel, just as he had opened the first. He and his disciples hesitate about the meaning of Jesus' mission. Jesus takes occasion of this to condemn the people's unbelief. Next he curses the towns of Galilee; in prophetic style he proclaims that revelation is only granted to the meek. The Pharisees come on the scene: two controversies lead up to the grave accusation of demoniacal magic, made specific on the occasion of the cure of the blind-mute (12:24). Jesus takes his stand firmly against the Pharisees. He refuses the sign from heaven which they ask and threatens them with the

unique sign of his resurrection. Finally Jesus' relatives
themselves appear sceptical about him: he can now count
only on the loyalty of his disciples. We are now able to
understand the bearing of the teaching in parables.

The turning-point foreshadowed since the first scene of
the second act has now been reached. The parables of
Jesus are going to single out his disciples from the uncomprehending crowd. For these parables enshrine a secret
which cannot be discovered without the Master's teaching, and to know this secret, that the Kingdom of God
is established in a wholly inward manner, is the very
condition of receiving the Word of God in its life-giving
efficacy. It is not surprising that the setting of this discourse matches that of the Sermon on the Mount. Thus
ends the teaching in Galilee. The episode at Nazareth
fittingly concludes it: Jesus is rejected by his own. Judaism
has condemned itself.

In the second part of the Gospel Jesus leads the life of
an outlaw, only occasionally resuming contact with the
crowd. His disciples do not leave him again and he continues to reveal himself to them. We follow him in succession into a 'place apart', to Gennesaret, to the districts of
Tyre and Sidon, into the mountains, along the Sea of
Galilee, to the district of Magadan and to the neighbourhood of Caesarea Philippi. To this last stay belong some
episodes which are essential to the gospel story: Peter
confesses his faith that Jesus is the Messias and receives
the great promise symbolized by the name of 'Peter', by
which he will now be called. As if Jesus had only been
waiting for this act of faith, he reveals to his disciples for
the first time the shameful death which awaits him in
Jerusalem, to be followed by his resurrection. The Transfiguration continues the series of revelations about the
'Son of Man' and the series of episodes which began at

Caesarea Philippi concludes with a second warning of the Passion.

The discourse in Volume IV may be understood as the beginnings of a 'constitution', in which Christ legislates for his little messianic community. He insists on that humility which must inspire those who hold authority, and on the forgiveness of offences. The episodes in Judaea adumbrate rules for the life of the Church.

The departure for Jerusalem is marked by a third and last warning of the Passion. This last journey culminates in the triumphal entry into the city, after which Jesus reveals his authority in the Temple, from which he drives out the traders.

Events hurry on to a crisis. Various questionings, with parables alluding to the Passion and the divine judgment, and above all a new series of controversies, lead up to the last great discourse. This is the climax of Christ's teaching. The Pharisees are solemnly condemned and we now look to the end of time; the Son of Man will come on the clouds of heaven; the Passion begins.

In relation to this plan the infancy-gospel has a somewhat adventitious air, but it cannot be cut out of the present Gospel, because it obviously corresponds to the same theological interest which governs the story of the public life. The evangelist is at pains to repeat to us that our Lord's life is marked out by the Old Testament prophecies. 'All this was done that the scriptures of the prophets might be fulfilled': some such formula recurs monotonously some ten times, from 1:22 to 26:56. We are made to understand that for the Jews to be scandalized by such a Messias[10] was inexcusable, because the life of Jesus was what it had to be. There should have been no scandal as to the place if they were expecting the Messias

[10] 1 Cor. 1:22ff.

to reveal himself first at Jerusalem; no scandal about humiliation, no scandal about the Passion: all the prophecies had to be fulfilled.

It was in this scriptural spirit that the first two chapters of our Gospel were composed. A genealogy demonstrates the continuity of the two Testaments; an arithmetical reckoning of the number of generations (three by twice seven) leads up to Christ as to the perfecting of Jewish history.[11] The name of Jesus, his birth of Mary the Virgin, all this was foretold; the flight into Egypt and the massacre of the Innocents corresponds to the law of types, according to which the life of the Messias must reproduce the beginnings of Israel's history.

The infancy-gospel thus forms a perfect prelude to the Gospel. The solemn appearance of Jesus on the mountain in Galilee (in which men loved to recognize the Mount of the great sermon) is its natural conclusion; henceforth the Apostles are sent no longer, as at first, to the towns of Israel, but to the nations. They are to 'teach' all the commandments contained in the Gospel and Jesus will be with them, upholding his word with his divine power, until the consummation of the world.

Once one has grasped the profound unity which controls this drama of the first Gospel, it seems to me one cannot help agreeing with the judgment of the first generations of Christians—and with many others since them—who preferred it to Mark and Luke. Mark is an 'abbreviator' and all Luke's art, with his claims to historical order, cannot rival Matthew's admirable and effortless ease. Even if tradition provided the stones ready-hewn, the master-mason who placed the materials, guided by his memories and his theology, has erected a monument for all time.

[11] Mt. 1: 17

Out of what was originally the recital of Jesus' discourses and the narrative of his miracles and journeys Matthew has composed a poignant drama. Thanks to him, we know why the human ministry of Jesus was what it was: success, struggle, final defeat. We know too why it survived: it had sown the little seed of the Kingdom of Heaven in the earth. It fulfilled the prophecies.

3

If we had to give a title to St Matthew's Gospel we should call it the Gospel of the Kingdom of Heaven. Being specially dedicated to Jesus' teaching, it condenses it in the message of the Kingdom. The Sermon on the Mount opens with the Beatitudes, the charter which lays down the qualities required in the subjects of the Kingdom. It describes the new 'justice' which is to take the place of the 'justice' on which the old religion was built. It deepens the concept of this new 'justice' so that it will henceforth be known as perfection and holiness; it reveals religious dispositions unknown to the ancient world, detachment, humility, charity.

In the Kingdom, certain disciples are associated with the work of its foundation, and for them detachment means renunciation, in order to be free. They are 'missionaries' and must on no account be encumbered on the journey they have undertaken.

The Kingdom of Heaven has its own secret. It has the 'littleness' belonging to all that must live in obscurity and the 'depths'. The 'depths', in this connexion, are the inmost recesses of those souls which must surrender themselves to the Kingdom: none can understand this but the souls who are capable of depth.

The revelation of the secret therefore decides who are destined for the Kingdom. Mankind will be divided into two classes of men according to whether they understand and accept it or pass it carelessly by.

Thus from the preaching of the Kingdom there is born, here on earth, the class of the true disciples, those who have received the 'seed of the Kingdom' and form the 'Kingdom of Heaven' present on earth; within the human race there is to be a 'community' of disciples: it will be 'the Church'. The Gospel of the Kingdom is also the Gospel of the Church.

The destiny of its Founder coincides with that of the Kingdom and determines it. This too has its secret, shown in the title 'Son of Man'. It will be tragic: in the designs of God the Passion has to precede the final establishment of the Kingdom.

From the Gospel of St Matthew there stands out the shining figure of Christ the teacher of doctrine, the divine lawgiver, as he is shown in the mosaics of the apses of Byzantine basilicas. That figure dominates the Christianity of the early centuries and it was from Matthew's Gospel that they sought 'the words of the Lord Jesus, which he spoke when he taught us humility and spiritual courage'.[12]

4

We have had occasion to express our opinion briefly on the 'synoptic problem',[13] which is concerned with explaining the striking resemblances between our first three Gospels and their equally notorious differences. This problem, realized since the patristic age, has been the subject of innumerable studies since the eighteenth century. All possible hypotheses have been examined from every angle: the dependence of the Gospels on one

[12] 1 *Clem.* 13, 1 ff.; cf. *Did.* 8, 2; 15, 3–4
[13] Cf. L. Vaganay, *Le problème Synoptique* (*Bibliothèque de Théologie*, ser. III, 1), Paris, 1954

another; a primitive written gospel, of which our present Gospels are recensions; explanation by oral tradition or by groupings of short partial stories.

In 1832 Schleiermacher, interpreting in his own way the passage from Papias quoted above,[14] read into it the existence of a primitive document, soon to become known as the 'Logia', consisting entirely of the 'sayings' of Jesus. This obvious misinterpretation led the critics, after many vicissitudes, to the classic theory of the 'two sources' (Mark or proto-Mark, and the Logia), which still commands a consensus of opinion (perhaps rather from exhaustion than from profound conviction). Some Catholics, being urged by a decree of the Biblical Commission to respect patristic tradition, inaugurated a movement of return to the thesis that St Matthew's Gospel is the oldest. The legitimate distinction between the Aramaic version and its Greek interpretation enabled them, moreover, to agree to a greater extent with the pertinent arguments which prove that Mark has a certain literary priority over our Greek Matthew.

A few examples will show more clearly than any number of explanations how complicated the problem is. It is a double problem, according to whether one considers the order of the incidents, or the way they are recorded.

As to the order of the incidents, on a general framework which is clearly the same for all, countless divergences are grafted. To take a single case, Matthew places the mission before the parable discourse, but Mark and Luke invert this order.

This same complication of likenesses and divergences is found in the versions of the different pericopes. We give an example chosen from many. Both the agreements and the variants of the formulas are quickly seen, even

[14] p. 7

in a translation, provided it sticks to the Greek and respects the order of the words.

MATTHEW 9: 14–15.	MARK 2: 18–20.	LUKE 5: 33–35.
Then come unto him John's disciples, saying:	Now the disciples of John and the Pharisees were fasting. And they come and say to him:	Now they [the Pharisees and their scribes] said unto him:
'Why do we and the Pharisees fast, while thy disciples do not fast?'	'Why do the disciples of John and the disciples of the Pharisees fast, while thy disciples do not fast?'	'John's disciples fast frequently and practise prayer, and so do those of the Pharisees, whereas thine do eat and drink.'
And Jesus said to them: 'Can the children of the bride-chamber mourn while yet the bridegroom is with them?	And Jesus said to them: 'Can the children of the bride-chamber fast while the bride-groom is with them? As long as they have the bridegroom with them they cannot fast.	Jesus said unto them, 'Can ye make the children of the bride-chamber fast while the bride-groom is with them?
'But the days shall come when the bridegroom shall be taken away from them, and then shall they fast.'	'But the days shall come when the bridegroom shall be taken away from them, and then shall they fast, in that day.'	'But the days shall come—and when the bridegroom shall be taken from them, then shall they fast, in those days.'

Our proposed solution of the synoptic problem has this advantage—and it is one—that it is more complex than the theory of two sources. It is more traditional, for it relies on the historical evidence of antiquity; it explains many matters of fact and corrects the excessive rigidity of the two-source theory, which up to a point we consider reasonable. It is put forward along the lines indicated by M. Goguel in his excellent study—one of the best there is—on the synoptic problem. 'We may consider', wrote this author, 'that the task now before criticism is, on the one hand, to define this theory accurately and, on the other, to explain, as far as this is possible, how the documents underlying the gospel literature were formed.'[15]

The other great problem, which we have also mentioned, is the historical value of St Matthew's Gospel. Loisy is specially severe: his difficulties include nearly all that the critics have ever been able to object against it. He writes:

> The evangelical matter in Matthew, so far as it consists of teachings, does not represent a single collection of memories faithfully preserved from the apostolic age, any more than its narratives represent the legend of Jesus in the same way. It contains rather a series of acquisitions successively taken over under the pressure of circumstance, of the progressive needs of Christian propaganda, and as required by the organization of Christian teaching in the communities.[16]

We have shown in Chapter One that the needs of the community were not incompatible with fidelity to the Master's teaching. Loisy continues: 'The original document was a *Didache* [a "teaching"] afterwards worked up into a gospel of the canonical type by amalgamation with Mark.'[17] That Matthew should be founded on a *Didache*

[15] *Introduction au Nouveau Testament*, t. I, Paris, 1923, p. 112
[16] *The Birth of the Christian Religion*, p. 47
[17] *Ibid.*

would certainly not lessen its value. But Loisy cannot conceive that a tradition could be reliable. Next come difficulties of detail:

> The narrative parts [of the first Gospel] are mainly founded on Mark, what is added to them being secondary fiction with apologetic bearings and sometimes romantically conceived, as in the role attributed to Pilate's wife in the story of the Passion. The birth-stories belong to the order of mythical fictions and are studiously elaborated in connexion with texts from the prophets.[18]

We hold on the contrary that Matthew is in direct contact with the primitive tradition, without passing through Mark. It is often richer than Mark. Pointing out the fulfilment of the Old Testament prophecies does not necessarily mean inventing the facts for the pleasure of conforming to the prophecies. A romantic touch, even if admitted as such—but who can draw the line between history and romance, except the witnesses?—would not affect the truth of the essential facts. We know too that a certain school classes every story of a miracle as 'mythical', but this is nothing but an outdated prejudice. Our generation of historians is less scared of the supernatural than their predecessors were.

We have not dealt with the problem of the authorship of our Greek Gospel. The Apostle Matthew could have supervised the Greek interpretation of his Aramaic Gospel, but this was not really necessary, if the apostolic Church made itself responsible for the new version. In point of fact, the apostolic Church did guarantee the truth, and consequently the value as an inspired book, of the Greek work: that is enough for us. It leaves us free to appreciate the difference, from a literary point of view, between an interpretation and a literal translation.

[18] *The Birth of the Christian Religion*, p. 46

To discuss the question of dates would take us too far. The time has long passed when one could relegate the writing of our Gospels to a date far on in the second century. The papyrus discoveries of recent years prove that the great 'four' were being read at Alexandria in their present text from the first quarter of the second century, and it must have taken some time for them all to be collected in that church. Now, of the four, the Gospel of Matthew, at least in its Aramaic edition, had the privilege of priority. This privilege, as we have shown, is shared by the Greek Gospel, which is no mere creation of the Hellenistic Christians of Syria, but follows in the wake of a primitive Matthew, first in Aramaic, then turned into Greek in Palestine. Thus we are brought back to the chronological datum provided by St Irenaeus, who dates the literary activity of St Matthew in the period of the apostolic preaching, 'while Peter and Paul were preaching the gospel in Rome and founding the church there'.

CHAPTER THREE

The Gospel According to Saint Mark

I T was St Augustine's belief that Mark's intention was to abridge the Gospel of Matthew. Was he right? We shall have to say a word about the author before going on to his work.

I

In the book of the Acts, in the Pauline Epistles and also in the tradition of the Church, we have a documentation of the evangelist which might almost be called abundant. John, surnamed Mark, was a very well-known personage in the Christian communities. John was his Jewish name; his surname of Mark—a Latin *praenomen* in Greek form—suggests to us a Graeco-Oriental background, and Mark belonged in fact to the Hellenist group in the Jerusalem community. He was related to Barnabas and perhaps, like him, a native of Cyprus and a Levite. His mother, Mary, lived in a large house in Jerusalem. The servant-girl was called Rhoda. Clearly we are well informed. The 'stump-fingered man',[1] as he was sometimes called in the communities, was a Christian of the very first generation. Still young at the time of his conversion, he lived in intimate association with Peter, Barnabas, Paul and Luke. But for a passing coolness with St Paul, no one had anything but good to speak of him. 'He was one of those admirable men', says Fr Lagrange,

---

[1] A nickname preserved by tradition: Hippolytus, *Philos.* VII, 30, 1; *Anti-Marcionite Prologue*.

'who shine in the second rank, or rather, who refrain from shining in order to devote themselves to greater personalities, thereby winning for themselves both the merit of modesty and a more fruitful if less personal activity.'[2]

Mark travelled first with Barnabas and Paul, then with Barnabas alone. Could he have gone with the latter as far as Alexandria? This hypothesis would at least explain the old traditions of the Egyptian church. Was it the premature death of Barnabas that suggested his going to rejoin St Peter, to preach the gospel with him to the church at Rome? He served the Prince of the Apostles as catechist; he recorded his instructions.

When Peter was reproducing the common tradition, when he was telling gatherings in Rome about the raising of Jairus' daughter, or how the devils were driven out at Gerasa, and the old oral tradition lived again on his lips, Mark would note down an Aramaic word which recurred to the Apostle's memory, or some picturesque touch which coloured the story. The Apostle had certain favourite stories, more personal to himself, like the walk that sabbath day at Capharnaum, the day after he had left his boat to follow Jesus. Mark took note of it all.

According to Papias, John 'the Elder' was accustomed to recall the circumstances in which Mark wrote in his Gospel:

> Mark, who had been Peter's interpreter, wrote down accurately, but not in order, all that he [Peter] remembered of what the Lord had said or done. For Mark had not heard the Lord, and had not been his disciple, but he had later been Peter's, as I said. Peter used to give his teaching according to the needs of the moment, without meaning to give the Lord's teachings in order, so that

[2] *Évangile selon saint Marc* (Paris, 1929), p. xix

Mark was not at fault when he wrote down some things just as he remembered them. He was only concerned for one thing: to omit nothing he had heard and to report nothing but the truth.[3]

Some have supposed that the 'Elder' was here showing his preference for the order of the Fourth Gospel. The context of Papias' work suggests, on the contrary, the Gospel of Matthew, whose good order is so praised. We can well understand this: to a man like Papias, chiefly interested in Christ's teachings, it would appear much better ordered than that of Mark.

Clement of Alexandria echoes a tradition according to which Mark published his Gospel while the Apostle Peter was still alive. Eusebius, to whom we owe this information, harmonized it with that given by Papias. Eusebius writes:

So brightly shone the light of piety in the minds of Peter's hearers, that they refused to be satisfied with a momentary hearing and the oral teaching of the divine message; in every way they set about begging Mark (whose Gospel we possess, and who was Peter's companion) and urging him to leave them in writing a lasting record of the teaching they had received by word of mouth. They refused to give him any peace till they had got their way, and thus became the cause of Mark's writing the Gospel which bears his name. They say that the Apostle learned what was going on by a revelation of the Spirit, and was pleased with this zeal, and sanctioned the Gospel with his authority to serve as the basis of the teaching in the churches. Clement states the facts in the sixth book of the Hypotyposes, and Papias, bishop of Hierapolis, agrees with him.[4]

[3] Eusebius, *H.E.*, III, 39, 15. Only the first sentence comes from 'the Elder'. The rest is an explanation by Papias.

[4] *H.E.*, II, 15, 2

St Irenaeus claimed to know that Mark only wrote later, 'after the martyrdom (departure) of Peter and Paul'.[5] In this he agrees with the anti-Marcionite Prologue, from which he perhaps borrowed the phrase. It could be understood in a broad sense. In reality it was only after the death of the Prince of the Apostles that Mark's Gospel was called in to take the place of Peter's oral teaching and had such a success. By its means, Peter being dead yet spoke, with a still living voice. But there is nothing to prevent us believing that Mark had long before written down his master's catechesis and that copies of his work were circulating in Rome.

It was a sort of first rough draft of his Gospel. Later he would have published an official edition. He would have added the ending we now read in a certain number of versions of his text—not in all, nor the most ancient— which is certainly later than St Luke's Gospel. Is it possible that Irenaeus' statement refers to this very last stage of the compilation of the text?

2

To appreciate the criticism of Mark made by 'the Elder', we have only to try to elucidate the plan of his Gospel. Loisy certainly exaggerates when he talks about 'all this amalgam of miracles and instructions, . . . this pile of memoirs',[6] which make up the second Gospel. All the same, the order is far from perfect.

It is generally agreed that two parts should be distinguished in the public life, with the messianic confession at Caesarea Philippi marking a definite turning-point. The following is the scheme we would suggest, disregarding minor divisions of the text and emphasizing the close

[5] *Ibid.*, V, 8, 3
[6] Loisy, *L'Évangile selon Marc* (Paris, 1912), p. 9

relations between the plans of the first two Gospels. (Roman figures indicate the main sections, corresponding to Matthew's 'volumes'.)

FIRST PART: The preaching in Galilee.

I. (1) Initial trilogy (1: 2–13).
   (2) Preaching in Galilee, call of disciples, day at Capharnaum, cure of a leper (1: 14–45).
   (3) Controversies with Pharisees. Summarized sketch of the preaching (showing up the great omission of the Sermon on the Mount) and miracles of Jesus; *choice of the Twelve*; another controversy; the brethren of Jesus (2: 1–3: 35).

II. (1) The Parables (4: 1–34).
   (2) Series of great miracles on the lake (4: 35–5: 43).

III. (1) Jesus at Nazareth, *mission of the Twelve* (with the missionary discourse); death of John the Baptist (6: 1–29).
   (2) *Return of the Twelve*, prelude to first multiplication of the loaves and the miracle of walking on the water (6: 30–56).
   (3) Arrival of Scribes from Jerusalem; great anti-Pharisee section (7: 1–23).

SECOND PART: From the break with Galilee.

IV. (1) Tyre and Sidon. The deaf-mute. Second multiplication of loaves; anti-Pharisee section; the blind man at Bethsaida (7: 24–8: 26).
   (2) *Caesarea Philippi*. Peter's confession; first warning of the Passion; Transfiguration; exorcism (8: 27–9: 29).

(3) *Incognito in Galilee.* Second warning of the Passion. Discourse on the first place and other sayings (9: 30–50).

V. (1) *Judaea and Peraea.* Questions by the Pharisees about marriage. The children. The rich young man (10: 1–31).

(2) *Going up to Jerusalem.* Third warning of the Passion. Question by James and John. Bartimaeus. Entry into Jerusalem. Traders driven from the Temple (scene set within the episode of the withered fig-tree) (10: 32–11: 26).

(3) Long questionings. Condemnation of the Pharisees, and the widow's mite (11: 27–12: 44).

(4) Great eschatological discourse (13: 1–37).

THIRD PART: The consummation.

The Passion (14: 1–15: 47).
The Resurrection (16: 1–20).

This purely literary and geographical division corresponds with a division in the design of the Gospel. Fr Lagrange brings it to light by distinguishing two stages in Jesus' preaching: the first, public preaching in Galilee; the second, a period of teaching, reserved for the disciples and bearing chiefly on the person of the Messias. 'In the first part, Jesus preaches the gospel, and preaches it in a way his hearers could understand, by means of parables. But this public teaching is, strictly speaking, only a bare outline of the gospel. Later on it will be revealed to all men. First it has to be explained more clearly to a few who will have the task of preaching it publicly.'[7]

What we have called the 'break with Galilee' is precisely the moment when Jesus devotes himself to training his disciples and revealing to them the 'secrets' of his

[7] *Évangile selon saint Marc* (Paris, 1929), p. lxiv

person. Fr Lagrange prefers to draw attention to the confession at Caesarea, as revealing the new orientation of Christ's teaching method.

A new period opens when Jesus lets himself be recognized as the Messias by Peter and his comrades, but only on condition that they really understand what sort of Messias he is. If we set aside an *introduction* in which John the Baptist announces the coming of a baptizer greater than himself, and Jesus, being baptized, receives his mission from heaven (1: 1–13), then the first part of the Gospel extends from 1: 14 to 8: 26. The wandering begins at the point where Jesus requires his disciples to think, not now of the Kingdom of God, but of himself.[8]

The second part of the Gospel, from the departure for Tyre and Sidon, agrees in general with the corresponding sections of the first Gospel both in content and in the order of events. This is by no means so with the first part. Because of the great omission of the Sermon on the Mount, miracles and exorcisms are necessarily more prominent than teaching—a fact which gives the Gospel of Mark a bent all its own. When we see how St Mark has elaborated the account of the day at Capharnaum we at once think of Peter's influence. Further, by his editorial arrangement, the evangelist has separated the choice of the Twelve from the missionary charge. Between these two he has interpolated the parable section, greatly developed. On the whole we prefer Matthew's order. The teaching method of the parables already marks the break with the crowd: this is no longer the time to launch a great mission proclaiming the Kingdom.

Another result of the omission of the Sermon on the Mount is that the controversies with the Pharisees are

[8] *Ibid.*, pp. lxiv ff.

reported at the very beginning of the public life. Here too, Matthew's perspective is preferable.

3

Was Mark, who owes so much to St Peter, also influenced by St Paul?

Ancient tradition, as we have seen, is silent on the subject. But the moderns have discovered in the Gospel of Mark a latent theology under the aegis of St Paul. Let us examine the case.

At the centre of St Matthew's Gospel is the doctrine of the Kingdom of God. The growth of the 'good news', the foundation of the Kingdom of God, started from the message of Jesus. This view is drawn from the actual course of the facts.

From the beginning of his Gospel St Mark draws attention to Jesus, to his being the Messias and to his quality as Son of God; the message of the Kingdom and the teaching take a second place. This is a fresh point of view. Is this simply the result of the way St Peter taught, because he liked telling and recalling the impression produced by Jesus' miracles? Or does it rather spring from some deeper reflection, from a 'theology' in which St Mark shows himself the disciple of St Paul?

We cannot answer this question without touching on what has been called, since a celebrated study of Wrede's,[9] 'the messianic secret' of St Mark's Gospel.

Before going on to this story, we should examine the traces of this mysterious 'secret' in the Gospel. They can be reduced to three categories:

(1) The silence imposed, in the first part of the Gospel, on the devils and the sick who were healed: on the possessed man at Capharnaum (1: 25); on the possessed

[9] *Das Messiasgeheimnis in den Evangelien* (Göttingen, 1901)

in general (1: 34); on the leper (1: 44–45); on the possessed again (3: 11–12). But in contrast Jesus commands the demoniac at Gerasa, after his cure, to go and tell his people about his cure (in the Decapolis). St Mark has generalized and thereby heightened the force of the words of Jesus which belong to the common tradition. It is perfectly natural that Jesus should not want the devils to proclaim him Son of God. They are undesirable witnesses. On the other hand, at least in Galilee, he desires to curb the enthusiasm of the crowd, which would have prevented him accomplishing a mission of any depth. In the Decapolis he has not the same scruples, and with good reason.

(2) The silence of the three witnesses at the time of the raising of Jairus' daughter (5: 43), and of the Transfiguration (9: 9). The motive for secrecy would seem to be different in the two cases: again to avoid the enthusiasm of the crowd in the first, and in the second to reveal a mystery to the privileged three.

(3) In the second part, the journeys *incognito*; and the silence imposed on the sick and the disciples. The silence in connexion with the miracles (7: 36, 8: 26) must be explained as in the first part, and also, no doubt, the silence required from the disciples as to Jesus being the Messias (8: 30). The meaning of the *incognito* has another bearing. Partly, no doubt, it is because Jesus wants to withdraw from the uncomprehending crowd and often, again, to avoid dangerous ovations, but also he desires solitude in order to train his Apostles. This last motive is confirmed by the evangelist himself (9: 30–31): 'They passed through Galilee, and he wished none to know; for he was teaching his disciples'; the subject of this teaching was the passion and the resurrection.[10]

---

[10] We do not here refer to the teaching in parables, which belongs to the common tradition. Mark is not involved.

If this short analysis has succeeded in showing that Mark likes to speak of 'secrecy', it equally reveals that tradition provided him with all the elements he has set in relief. Jesus' horror of being confessed by the devils, his fear of the crowd's enthusiasm, his desire to escape temporarily from the persecutions of the Pharisees and Herod Antipas, and his desire to have his Apostles with him (cf. 3: 14) so as to train them, all these are features retained by the primitive tradition and they are only natural.

The theories built up on this are too one-sided. St Mark is supposed to have imagined for himself that Jesus wanted to hide his quality of Messias (Wrede). Or again —a theory more in vogue today—he wanted to present Jesus as Son of God, but in 'secret epiphanies' (Dibelius). Fr Lagrange thinks for his part that the 'secrecy' was chiefly concerned with the doctrine of Christ's death and resurrection.

The truth seems to us more complicated. The intentions which explain the 'secrecy' are complex, and they come from Jesus himself. They correspond to the enforced necessities of a Messias who willed to be a purely religious Messias, one whose ministry was carried out in the midst of a superstitious, fanatical and nationalist people, one who encountered opposition and undesirable contacts on his way. Knowing that he had to fulfil the messianic figure of the 'Servant of God' as depicted by Isaias, Jesus had to accustom his disciples to this point of view; he could only do it in a 'secret' course of teaching, which must obviously contain the germ of a theology.

We can now, however, form a better estimate of the sort of elaboration to which St Mark has subjected the common tradition. *Under Peter's influence* he has made the story of events, and especially of miracles,

predominant in his Gospel. He obtained this result in
particular by eliminating part of Christ's teachings and
by clothing the traditional narratives in that lively and
picturesque form they received from the lips of St Peter.
Apart from some episodes of the 'day at Capharnaum',
Peter's catechesis at Rome does not seem to have greatly
enriched the common tradition. That is understandable,
for already, in Jerusalem, Peter had been present at its
birth.

Paul's influence, we are told, is strongly marked in
both the style and the theology. But except in the
canonical conclusion, where some Pauline touches must
certainly be admitted, St Mark's style is always that of
the common tradition.

As we have just seen, in the supposed theology of the
messianic secret, gratuitously ascribed to Paul's influence,
there is nothing which does not derive from pre-existing
tradition. The emphasis on the death and resurrection of
Christ, if we must connect it with theology, developed in
the primitive community independently of the Apostle;
the mystery of the parables, which should obviously be
compared with the mystery of the Wisdom of God in
St Paul, is a theme which belongs to the apocalyptic
tradition, and is fully in place in the teaching of Jesus
and the first apostolic catechesis.

4

Recent criticism accepts the priority of Mark as a
dogma: the two other synoptic Gospels must have copied
him. This did no harm, so long as the critics stoutly
maintained the historical truth of the story and connected
it with the teaching of Peter. That was the line of the
Liberal Protestant school.

But then came Wrede. We have alluded to his thesis

concerning the messianic secret in the Gospels, especially in the Gospel of St Mark. If the theory of the messianic secret applies in particular to Mark, the first of the evangelists, then the tradition, the whole tradition, can only be accessible to us now mixed with a theology and elaborated by it. This leads to saying that the theology has created the tradition. Errors take their inevitable course; it would take too long to trace the stages of their path, which forks more than once.

One of the points they reach is the last position taken up by Loisy. Worship has replaced theology as the centre of interest, and the earliest of the Gospels in date, that of Mark, has become the first ritual of the Christian mystery, the first 'catechism of the worship rendered to the Lord Christ'.[11]

Two cycles, or centres, are discernible, the cycle of the preaching in Galilee and the cycle of the passion in Jerusalem; the instruction of catechumens and the revelation of a mystery; the baptismal catechism and the eucharistic. The whole is thus brought into co-ordination with the great rites of Christian initiation and with the Christian mystery.[12]

Loisy pursues this theme:

Mark seems to have been a Roman Gospel of ancient date. Its attribution to Mark possibly coincides with the final revision of the book and the introduction of the Sunday Easter, when the Roman community ceased to celebrate the festival of salvation on the same day as the Jews. . . . On this we may remark, but only as a probable hypothesis, that the revision of Mark, with its characteristic ill will to these Galilean Apostles was the work of parties in Rome devoted to the memory of Paul, and

11 *The Birth of the Christian Religion*, p. 43
12 *Ibid.*

was finally adopted, with the observance of the Sunday Easter, when the Roman community became united towards the beginning of the second century.[13]

But how, in point of fact, are our Gospels in the least like 'manuals' of worship? We could easily imagine these manuals of eucharistic worship: the *First Epistle of St Clement of Rome*, the *Teaching of the Apostles*, the *Martyrdom of Polycarp*, even St Paul's 'captivity' Epistles, show us what the style of the ancient liturgies was like: it was utterly different from the style of our synoptic Gospels. To say that the story of the Passion was written for the pleasure of introducing a Paschal date is simply farcical. As for the ill will of 'Paulinism' in Roman circles against Peter (that hackneyed old theory of the school of Baur), we have only to read the praise of the Apostles in the same *Epistle of Clement of Rome*, at the end of the first century. The tradition of the Church unites the memory of the two Apostles in its devotion, there in Rome. So when were these stories of ill will elaborated? Sincerity is not ill will.

It must be added that their very excesses condemn all those methods which only exclude from their field of vision one single hypothesis: namely, that *tradition* might well be among Christians what it was in Judaism and what it is everywhere, the memory of what a master has taught. Perhaps the abuse of theories will lead back some day to a respect for history.

[13] *The Birth of the Christian Religion*, p. 46

CHAPTER FOUR

The Book of Saint Luke

Wﬂﬂ the work of St. Luke, the gospel tradition embarks on its career as literature. Matthew and Mark were content to write down the 'good news'; their Gospels were still essentially the apostolic message: history indeed, for the message included the miracles and teaching of Jesus of Nazareth, but first and foremost preaching. Matthew and Mark are not historians but evangelists. St Luke claims to write as an historian of Christianity, and from that angle we shall read his Gospel. Our attention will be struck by another characteristic of the book: Luke, the historian carefully collecting his facts, has discovered a whole mine of information not worked by the tradition of the Twelve, which he owes to early 'disciples' of Jesus.

I

Like Polybius, who saw the dawn of Rome's fortunes and told us the story of its birth, this disciple of Paul had the vision of a powerful religious movement which was to change the destinies of the empire, and wrote, for posterity, the book of the Christian beginnings. The story of Jesus was to form the first volume, the history of the Church's growth the second. Both were dedicated to Theophilus, a prominent Christian in the Graeco-Roman world.

He considers two duties to be incumbent on anyone producing an historical work: to write an 'ordered'

narrative and to go to the sources. He describes this
method of his in the prologue which, in the manner of
ancient authors, he sets at the head of his first book:

> Inasmuch as many have attempted to put together an
> account of the things that have been fulfilled amongst us,
> even as the original eye-witnesses and ministers of the
> word delivered them to us, it hath seemed good to me
> also, who have followed up all things carefully from
> the beginning, to write for thee an orderly account
> thereof, Excellent Theophilus, in order that thou mayest
> realize the certainty of the words wherein thou wast
> instructed.

Thus we pass out of the sphere of religious instruction
and tradition into that of history.

His concern to produce an historical work appears here
and there, for example in the well-known synchronizing
at the beginning of Christ's public life: 'In the fifteenth
year of the reign of Tiberius Caesar, when Pontius Pilate
was governor of Judaea,' etc. The author's style, too,
when he is not controlled by respect for the documents,
is eminently worthy of the historian's art.

Who, then, is this historian, included in the list of the
evangelists?

We have called him Luke. The tradition of the Church
(Irenaeus, Tertullian, the anti-Marcionite Prologue to
the Gospels) is unanimous in naming as the author of the
third Gospel this disciple and travelling companion of
St Paul, 'the beloved physician' of whom the Apostle
speaks in his Epistles.[1] Here and there we may glean a
few other pieces of information for a biography of the
writer: that he was perhaps a citizen of Antioch in Syria,
that he wrote his Gospel for the Corinthians and that

[1] Col. 4: 14; Philem. 24; 2 Tim. 4: 11

Paul took him with him as legal adviser for his trial in Rome.

Thus speaks tradition. If we analyse the two books to Theophilus, we are led from that angle too to attribute them to St Luke. The argument proceeds with almost mathematical rigour. The author of certain sections of the Acts (the 'we' sections) must be one of St Paul's companions who were with him on those voyages where the author writes 'we': this can only be Luke. Considering that the style is the same throughout, the author of the 'we' sections must be the author of the whole book. Furthermore, the similarity of style and procedure, as well as the way the prologues fit into each other, obliges us to say that the author of the Acts is also the author of the Gospel.

In Greek society a physician was a person of standing. His profession was one of the liberal arts; his colleagues were made much of in the courts of kings and pensioned by the famous Museum (the University) of Alexandria. Hippocrates and the school of Cos had shed a genuine scientific lustre on the profession. Many doctors in antiquity led a cosmopolitan life, living as *metics* (foreign residents) in the Greek cities, venturing all on their good fortune. Luke's good fortune was to meet an outstanding client in the person of Paul and to attach himself to him. We need not then be surprised to find in Paul's company a doctor who is fond of travelling, a professed historian and possibly a jurist.

Some very reputable authors, like Hobart and Harnack, believe they can prove that the language of Luke's two books is that of a doctor. It is rather interesting that the non-scriptural prologue which most resembles that of Luke is precisely that of a medical work, the treatise on medicine by the Greek Dioscorides, an army doctor under Claudius.

At what point should we date the literary activity of this doctor-historian? The abrupt conclusion of the Acts suggests that it must have been written at the time when the Apostle's Roman captivity was ending, which in all probability was in A.D. 63. Harnack laid much stress on this conclusion and the Biblical Commission itself requires us to take it into consideration.

The Gospel is earlier than the book of the Acts. Should we agree with the anti-Marcionite Prologue that it was published in Achaea? From Rome to Corinth is not so very far. But for this authority, we should say that Luke took advantage of the long captivity in Rome to put his notes in order and compose his Gospel in Rome.

2

In writing a gospel, St Luke was bound by the tradition as well as by his own sources and he had the honesty to follow them both closely. Consequently his work is still in the line of Matthew and Mark, with the addition of some new features.

At the same time he had the tact to retain the 'gospel' style. Even his language proves this.

He has tried to write in purer Greek without changing any of the original meaning, especially as regards the sayings of Jesus, and so well has he done it that even under his Greek we can recognize that subsoil of Aramaic which is the very stuff of the primitive catechesis. Moreover we can recognize it as clearly in the parts peculiar to himself. He must then have always followed the same plan, as an honest man who wants to give the facts as they are, and a Greek who knows how to handle his language.[2]

[2] M.-J. Lagrange, *Évangile selon saint Luc* (Paris, 1921), p. ciii

For the Acts, Luke had no model in the Christian world: it is therefore to this book we must turn first, to ascertain his method. We can see that it has two main parts. The beginning tells the story of the community at Jerusalem and its first mass-movements in Judaea and Samaria. This brings us to the foundation of the church in Antioch, the event on which so much hinges (Acts 1–13). From Antioch Paul sets out on his apostolic conquests, which form the second part of the book, telling of the Apostle's journeyings up to his captivity in Rome.

Into this general framework are fitted the documents he has collected. Luke generally confines himself to copying them accurately, arranging them in geographical and chronological order (this perfectly suits the subject of his book, which is the progress of Christianity) and fitting them together with remarks of a general nature. He possesses written sources of considerable extent: a description of the primitive community in Jerusalem, the Acts of Philip, the Acts of Peter and his own travelling diary. He has also many personal notes collected in the course of his contacts with those 'early disciples' whom he has visited. Reading him carefully, we realize both the wealth of his documentation and the care he has taken to preserve their literal content. It is marvellous to see what a work of art he has made out of all this jumble of material.

The plan of the public life in the Gospel is parallel to that of the Acts. The second part is the story of a journey, our Lord's great journey to Jerusalem. Luke found the subject in his sources but gave it a new importance. The first part describes the progress of Christ's mission in Galilee.

As a guide to our observations, let us first draw up a rather detailed plan of the Gospel.

Literary prologue (1: 1–4).

Prologue: The parallel childhoods of John the Baptist and Jesus (1: 5 to 2: 52).

FIRST PART: The evangelization of Galilee.

I. (1) Initial trilogy (3: 1–4: 13).
   (2) Nazareth. Capharnaum (the day there). The lake of Gennesaret. Miraculous draught of fishes and call of first four disciples (4: 14–5: 11).
   (3) *Section borrowed from Mark,* from the cure of the leper (Mk. 1: 40) to the choosing of the Twelve (Mk. 3: 19); miracles and controversies (5: 12–6: 11).
   (4) Sermon on the Plain; here, Luke follows *Matthew's tradition* (6: 12–49).
   (5) Capharnaum, the centurion (Mt.). Naim. John's disciples. (Mt.) Anointing by the sinful woman (7: 1–50).
II. (1) Great evangelistic tour. Jesus accompanied by the Twelve and the women of Galilee. The Parables. Jesus' kinsfolk (8: 1–21).
   (2) *Section borrowed from Mark,* from calming the storm, Mk. 4: 35 to Mk. 5: 43, i.e. journey beyond the lake; the great miracles (demoniac at Gerasa, woman with issue of blood, Jairus' daughter) (8: 22–56).
III. (1) Mission of the Apostles. Herod the Tetrarch. Return of the Apostles. Multiplication of the loaves (9: 1–17). (*Luke's great mission,* corresponding to Mk. 6: 45–8: 26.)
   (2) Peter's confession, first warning of the Passion, Transfiguration, exorcism. Second warning of the Passion. The 'first place' (9: 18–50).

SECOND PART: The great journey to Jerusalem, at first *proper to Luke* (to 18: 14).

I. (1) In Samaria. Call of disciples. Mission of the Seventy-two (with missionary discourse). The curse on the towns. Return of the disciples (9: 51–10: 24).

(2) The good Samaritan. Martha and Mary. On prayer (10: 25–11: 13).

(3) Against the Pharisees. The great accusation; a meal with a Pharisee; discourse to disciples and the crowd. Incidents, parables, various sayings (11: 14–13: 21).

II. (1) The journey to Jerusalem recalled. Succession of discourses (13: 22–35).

(2) Meal with a Pharisee on the sabbath. Parables on mercy. On riches. Parable of the clever steward. The rich man and Lazarus. Miscellaneous injunctions (14: 1–17: 10).

III. (1) The journey again resumed. The ten lepers. Apocalyptic discourse. Parables: the widow and the judge; the Pharisee and the Publican (17: 11–18: 14).

(2) Continuation of the journey to Jerusalem, in which *Luke resumes the plan of Mark (and Matthew)*, with the usual incidents, from the blessing of the children. Additional incidents: Zacchaeus at Jericho; Jesus weeps over Jerusalem (18: 15–19: 48).

IV. (1) The great questionings (20: 1–21: 4).

(2) The eschatological discourse (21: 5–38).

THIRD PART: The consummation.

The Passion (22: 1–23: 56).
The Resurrection (appearance to the holy women; to the disciples at Emmaus; the Ascension) (24: 1–53).

Luke's self-assigned task of writing an ordered history was less easy for the Gospel than for the Acts. An author with less respect for his sources might perhaps have had more success; Luke's sources, already resembling 'Lives' of Jesus, bound him to their viewpoint while often disturbing his literary design.

As his main sources St Luke possessed Mark and one or more other narratives resembling our Gospel of Matthew. It is hard to say in what state he knew the Matthaean tradition. He does not seem to have had our present Greek Matthew at his disposal. We may well suppose that for the general arrangement of his story he would have preferred Mark, which gave more of the impression of a life of Jesus. But when one thinks how Luke always liked to keep close to his sources, the hypothesis that he knew our first Gospel involves some phenomena difficult to explain. In some passages he agrees with it word for word; in others it looks like two different translations from the same original. Then again, in St Luke's Gospel the Matthaean material is found broken up. While Luke only rarely changes the order of episodes from Mark, he does so regularly for the matter which is common to him and Matthew. Moreover in the sections parallel with the second Gospel he never inserts episodes from his own special documents; the pericopes springing from the Matthaean tradition, on the contrary, usually alternate with passages belonging to his own sources—he never follows a Matthaean track for long.

It is therefore safer to suppose that he did not possess our Greek Matthew as we now have it, but that he knew several of those partial translations mentioned by Papias, which preceded the publication of the complete Gospel. The 'attempts' of which Luke speaks in his prologue might well be some of these partial translations.

Besides Mark's Gospel and the gospel 'attempts' which preceded our present Matthew, Luke possesses information of his own which is of particular interest and charm.

An historical biography of Jesus necessarily begins with memories of his childhood. Luke has conceived the original idea of parallel childhood stories, interweaving the biography of John the Baptist with that of Jesus.

The first part of the narrative, viewed as an evangelization of Galilee, is constructed on the plan of the first two Gospels. As regards the incidents, Luke is content to add to them the stories of the raising of the young man from the dead at Naim and the conversion of the woman who was a sinner. It amounts to very little and we may say that in substance he merely reads Mark and the Matthaean tradition in synopsis. But he has imposed his own 'order' on them.

After the initial trilogy, a geographical reference appears: from Nazareth, Jesus' home town, where the message is begun, we are transported to Capharnaum, then to the Lake of Gennesaret. The geographical plan reappears after the Sermon on the Plain; Capharnaum, Naim, then a long evangelizing tour. But his sources do not allow Luke to keep up the plan; he borrows whole sections from Mark in which the geographical order is not visible.

His chief debt to Matthew is the Sermon on the Plain (the Sermon on the Mount). We need not split hairs over the difference of scene. Both evangelists are right. Jesus addressed the crowd on countless occasions, sometimes on a hill, sometimes on the plains, sometimes on the shores of the lake. Luke could perfectly well set it on a plain in Galilee.

This freedom of composition allows the evangelist to insert into the course of his story little touches, such as

those precious details which introduce the parables: Jesus
went through all the towns and villages in Galilee,
preaching the good tidings, with the Twelve and the holy
women whom he had cured; Mary, called the Magda-
lene; Joanna, wife of Chuza, Herod's steward; Susanna
and many others, who ministered to the needs of the
apostolic band. We may note in passing that this Mary,
whom Luke knew well and whom Jesus had delivered
from 'seven demons', may possibly be the unknown
woman who anointed him. Luke is very tactful.

Some are surprised to find no trace in our Gospel of
the second multiplication of the loaves. But this follows
simply from the plan on which he composed it. Luke's
scheme did not allow for Jesus' journey in the district of
Tyre and Sidon: after the evangelization of Galilee, they
must leave for Jerusalem. So the incidents of the journeys
outside Galilee had to be dropped, except for the essential points: Peter's confession, the Transfiguration and
the warnings of the Passion.

The most interesting part of Luke's Gospel, because it
has no counterpart in Matthew and Mark, is the story
of the evangelizing on the way to Jerusalem. Here Luke
shows his powers as an historian, not so much in the
chronological or geographical arrangement of the events
as in the wealth of his information and the portrait of
Christ which emerges from it.

In the course of his own journeys Luke met many
disciples who did not belong to the group of the Twelve.
He was curious enough to question also the women of
Galilee—Mary, Joanna and Susanna: from these con-
versations he drew the impression that there existed a
gospel somewhat different from that of the Twelve
(Matthew and Mark): a gospel of the disciples. And he
has given us a conspectus of the contents of this gospel

by depicting a long evangelistic journey in the border district of Galilee, while Jesus was skirting Samaria on his way to Jerusalem. Let us entrust ourselves to him for the new perspective. In this second stage of his mission Jesus was recruiting new disciples and preparing for the time when Christianity would burst the narrow bounds of the little province of the Twelve. That is what the disciples told him.

At the beginning of this second part there is a general setting of the scene which copies the gospel of the Twelve. There are instances of individual disciples being called; then the appointment of the Seventy-two disciples—the number suggests the evangelization of the nations—and their sending out on a mission, together with a missionary discourse and the incident of their return. It is the counterpart of the corresponding episodes in the gospel of the Apostles. Then follows a long section dominated by various instructions and parables.

We should read again Luke's parables, masterpieces that they are. The parable of the good Samaritan—or rather of charity: the charity of the Samaritan is worth more than all the practices of the Priests and Levites. It illustrates the words 'I desire mercy and not sacrifice' (Mt. 9: 13; 12: 7). It is futile to accuse Luke of conceiving the Master's doctrine on the Pauline model; Jesus is always true to himself.

The parable of the merciful father (the prodigal son)— the gospel within the Gospel, as it has been called— throws light on the very notion of Godhead. God stoops to man if man becomes aware of his misery, and God is merciful. He loves his mercy more than his justice, more even than his sheer goodness, and Jesus is the reflection of this mercy.

The parable of the Pharisee and the publican: learn

here how to pray. The publican's humility responds to the divine mercy.

Other parables, such as the clever steward or the rich man and Lazarus, deal with the use of wealth and exalt poverty. It is well known that the communities in Jerusalem, especially the Hellenists, carried charity to the point of getting rid of their possessions. Poverty, together with humility and charity, had become a Christian virtue. Jesus had taught it, not only in the Sermon on the Mount but in the parables preserved by his disciples.

Thus we see our Lord's teaching based on mercy (God's and the Christian's), on confident prayer, on humility, on the good use of wealth. Dare we say that this goes beyond the religion of Jesus? The Sermon on the Mount already includes all these features, and some of Matthew's parables are already rough drafts of Luke's. The great difference lies in this, that in the Sermon on the Mount the Christian dispositions are demanded by the fundamental message of the Kingdom of God, whereas in the gospel of the disciples they are detached from this message and praised for their own sakes. In this sense there is progress. But two years have passed between the beginning of the public life and the mission on the borders of Galilee. The doctrine of the Galilean teacher has been stripped of the Jewish formulas which hedged it in; henceforth it expresses a universal religion, with the beliefs and virtues which will be at the root of Christianity.

3

Luke deserves to be treated and criticized as an historian. If he has transformed the gospel, it is not in order to insert a theology, even were it that of his master St Paul. Besides, it is clear from the Acts that he is not greatly interested in theology. The discussions on the

Law and justification do not excite him. As a Christian of the first generation, he does indeed value the manifestations of the Spirit very highly and has stressed their first appearances in the Gospel. He loves prayer and shows us Christ spending nights of prayer on the mountain. This is only accentuating some traits of the common tradition: it is scarcely a theology. He emphasizes evangelical poverty. But surely this is just what one would expect from a convert from paganism, who notices more clearly than the Apostles what is original in the Christian message.

Treating Luke as an historian, we must now ask ourselves the biggest question, which is the touchstone of his responsibility and respect for truth. This company of seventy-two disciples, is it his invention, or is it simply the synthesis of facts drawn from reliable sources?

From the Acts it is clear how interested Luke was in the 'early disciples' (the expression is his) whom he was able to know: Philip the evangelist, Cleophas and his companion, whom we now call the Emmaus disciples, the 'early disciple' Mnason of Cyprus (Acts 21: 16) and Manahen (Acts 13: 1). There can be no doubt that all these belonged to the Seventy-two. Barnabas, Stephen and others may also have been of the number. Remember the number of a hundred and twenty, given for the community at Pentecost; to make up this number we must add to the Twelve, the brethren of Jesus and the holy women, more than eighty names. Many went up with Jesus to Jerusalem; they formed a distinct group in the community, like the Twelve, the Lord's brethren and the women. They very probably formed the nucleus of those Hellenistic Christians who are mentioned in connexion with the choice of the seven deacons.

It is understandable that the common tradition (that

of the Twelve, the Galilean Apostles) did not make much of these disciples of the outer circle and attached little importance to the second period of evangelization, which abutted on the Samaritan world and even the Greek. The variance between Hellenists and 'Hebrew' Jews which came to light at the choice of the deacons is already foreshadowed in the gospel story.

Luke did not share the scruples of the common tradition and knew how to get his information. Since he proves himself perfectly dependable when he deals with the common tradition (that of the Twelve), where we can check him, we must allow him the same credit about the tradition of the disciples. I do not believe Luke ever invents; he has assembled his documentation from the disciples of Jesus. Why should this be suspect because it differs from the tradition of the Twelve and goes beyond it?

The benefit of these considerations will apply also to the infancy-gospel. Here we touch another circle of the primitive community: the Lord's brethren, his mother, the holy women of Galilee. These folk have their memories.

Luke makes it a point of courtesy to describe the appearances of the risen Christ only according to the recollections of the holy women and the disciples. Must we then say that he is ignorant of the more official appearances granted to the Apostles? Does he know nothing of what Paul taught the churches as the foundation of their faith, the appearance to Peter (though the Emmaus disciples learn of it at Jerusalem) and those to the Twelve, to James, and so on?

Goodwill is one of the gifts necessary for the historian, but many modern critics have lost it. There is much at stake here. If the gospel of the disciples is historical, it breaks the rigid bounds imposed by the common tradition; the living voice of the gospel is fuller than is supposed by those critics who would confine it all to the Gospel of Mark, in order to destroy it all with greater ease.

4

There is no lack of hypotheses about the second part of the public life. Some consider it a homogeneous source, parallel to Mark and the Logia, others as a first draft for a complete gospel which Luke later revised after he knew Mark's Gospel. It seems to us that the evangelist personally worked over the various memoirs to which he had access.

Loisy is at least as hard on Luke's work as on Matthew's. Not on Luke himself, whom he greatly respects, but on a so-called 're-caster' who has ruined for us the two volumes of the first history of Christianity. As for the re-cast Gospel: 'Mark has furnished most of the stories in the body of the book; what does not come from Mark is legendary fiction or mythical construction; examples of these are the preaching of Jesus at Nazareth, the mission of the seventy-two disciples, the Ascension of the risen Christ.'[3] Then the inevitable 'cult-book': 'The first book "to Theophilus" became a cult-book, impersonalized and enriched with the latest acquisitions of the faith.'[4] So that pearl of literature, the appearance to the disciples of Emmaus, is thus explained: it 'brings the Sunday Easter into full relief'![5] Excess of criticism has destroyed his literary and historical sense of touch.

None the less, Luke's work has found convinced champions among the critics, Harnack and Ramsay being the

---

[3] *The Birth of the Christian Religion*, p. 49
[4] *Ibid.*, p. 50
[5] *Ibid.*

most illustrious. Loisy's theory of re-casting cannot really stand against the impression of unity which is given by Luke's book: unity of method, of style and of language. When reaction sets in from the prejudice which sought to explain the supernatural element pervading all the historical memoirs of Jesus by the time and the remoteness of the evidence, then justice will be done to Luke, as it has been to Mark and the Logia of Matthew, and it will be admitted that in his two books we possess a reliable history of our origins. He will be read with the admiration which Loisy reserves for his 'primitive' writing:

> Luke has told us his method and his sources. He was careful to get direct information. He knew eye-witnesses of the gospel story and the actors in the apostolic story; he has questioned them; he has very exact personal memories for a considerable part of the apostolic story and makes use of them. If he does not stress the part which he has been able to draw from earlier writings, it is not to conceal the use he makes of them; it must be he supposed, rightly or wrongly, that they are founded on the direct evidence which he has used to check them. Although his witnesses were fanatics and he was not himself a critic of his own faith, his love of the truth, his soundness of judgment and a certain sense of reality had given him the ability to construct a work whose solidity, sincerity and impartiality are attested by the very care which has been taken to deprive us of its best parts.[6]

We may be very sure that the actual Luke would not have found favour with Loisy, if he had not had the luck to have the 're-caster' put in his place. Loisy's admiration is at bottom only a part of his sharp-eyed criticism, which has restored or invented an authentic Luke. If we must

[6] *Les Actes des Apôtres* (Paris, 1925), pp. 20–21

choose between the history which has been preserved and that which has been imagined, we prefer the former.

Much has been written about Luke's style. We cannot resist the temptation to quote a page of Aimé Puech, devoted to the praise of the evangelist.

What is much more interesting is that Luke has art, a delicate art, and all the more delicate in that it is usually, though not only, instinctive. In him already appears distinctly the new character of Christian art in all its forms: *soul*. With him everything is natural, alive and touching. Not that he aims at realism, properly speaking; in him, as in Matthew, many factual details given by Mark disappear or are blurred. His manner is wholly inward; he prefers psychology to the picturesque. He excels at discerning the secret movements of the heart and describing them with telling sobriety. He stirs us and moves us to compassion with a few discreet touches, all the more penetrating for their discretion. In the story of the young man who was raised at Naim, it is 'the *only* son' who is being carried out dead from his mother's house, and the mother is a *widow* (7: 12). A little later comes the phrase, 'and he *gave* him to his mother' (7: 15). In the parable of the Good Samaritan, there are those homely details: the 'oil' and the 'wine' which the charitable wayfarer pours on the wounds (10: 34); the 'mule' on which he takes the wounded man to the inn; the 'two shillings' he gives the host on leaving next morning (10: 35); in the parable of the prodigal son we have the 'swine' he tended in his want and the 'pods' he wished he could share with them (15: 16); his little talk with himself, so touching in its simplicity, where he avows his repentance (15: 18–20); the fatted calf which the father kills on his return (15: 23). All that is delightful, but surely the most persuasively delicate and irresistibly gracious of St. Luke's stories is the episode of the travellers to Emmaus. One ought really to quote it in full, from the first words—'And they were talking with one another over all these events, and it came to pass that whilst they were talking and discussing, Jesus himself drew nigh and went along with them' (24: 14–15)—down to the last: 'And they said one to another, Was not our heart burning within us whilst he spoke to us on the way, whilst he laid open to us the Scriptures?' (24: 32).

In these exquisite passages, even more than in the infancy-gospel, Luke reveals his whole self, with all his native delicacy, made yet more sensitive and attractive by the influence of Christ which he had so well absorbed. It is plain that however the facts may have been handed on to him by tradition, the form is here all his own. It is certainly not *invention*, at least not intentionally; Luke certainly had too much respect for the story he was telling to give way to the temptation to embellish it; his instinct for thought and feeling provide an *interpretation* of this story, deeper and truer than anything the shrewdest criticism could ever give it. It is *poetry* and *truth*.[7]

The reader may well regret that we have given so little rein to the admiration we rightly feel for the gospel literature. Is it altogether our fault if so many critics have done their best to damage these masterpieces of art and religion? If this is deplored, we have not written in vain.

[7] *Histoire de la Littérature Grecque Chrétienne*, I (Paris, 1928), pp. 115 ff.

CHAPTER FIVE

The Gospel of Saint John

THE fact that the Church has received and included in the number of the 'Four' a Gospel so different from the first three can best be explained if some authority—which can only be an *apostolic* authority—imposed it. Tradition indicates that this authority is that of John the Apostle, last survivor of the Twelve. There is therefore a Johannine problem, which criticism has examined in all its aspects. This Johannine problem, the relation of the Fourth Gospel to the synoptics, the theology of this Gospel—these are the points which interest us.

I

The first problem to be solved is that of the Apostle's survival and his sojourn in Ephesus.

Throughout the whole of the second century the churches of Asia were certain that John, the son of Zebedee and brother of James the Greater, had ended his days in peace at Ephesus, in extreme old age. They preserved the memory of this grand old man, the favourite disciple of Christ, who combined the character of an eye-witness of Christ with the dignity of a Jewish high priest: 'John, who rested on the bosom of the Lord; who was a high priest and wore the *petalon*, martyr and doctor'.[1] They venerated his tomb. The bishops of Asia, Polycrates of Ephesus (about 190), representing the tradition of seven bishops, and his relations Melito of Sardis

[1] Synodal letter of Polycrates, in Eusebius, *H.E.*, V, 24, 3

(about 160) and Polycarp of Smyrna (about 165), all with one accord echo the tradition. St Irenaeus, bishop of Lyons, as a young man had heard Polycarp discoursing on his intimate relations with the Apostle; he did not hesitate to recall this memory to Florinus, who had formerly shared his friendship with the bishop of Smyrna.[2]

Is it possible, as some critics suppose, that a tradition so definite and so widespread may be nothing but a delusion? We are told on the evidence of Papias of Hierapolis[3] that there was in Asia another John, a disciple of the Lord, who was very highly considered by the Elders of Asia. Might this not be the origin of a confusion in which the disciple took the place of the Apostle?

This hypothesis seems to gain some credit too from the title of 'disciple', so often attached to the name of John. But John could well have stuck to this title. It is the earlier title, and our synoptic tradition itself bears witness to the days when the Twelve were regularly called the Disciples. In certain circles the name of Apostle might well mean less than it means to us now, and we can easily imagine that the old Apostle, living his memories again, purposely chose the more archaic title of Disciple. Going beyond the Twelve, the group which had guided the infant church at Jerusalem, he reached back to the years of intimacy he had spent with our Lord. His rank of 'disciple' well bespoke the authority he possessed to speak in the Master's name and reveal his deeper thoughts.

Let us grant the possibility that at the end of the first century there lived in Asia two well-known Johns, John the Apostle, son of Zebedee, and John the disciple, the Elder. But we have no right, on the strength of Papias'

---

[2] Eusebius, *H.E.*, II, 20, 4–8
[3] See the passage quoted above, p. 7

somewhat ambiguous text, to cast doubt on a tradition as strong as that of the whole episcopate of Asia in the second century. And there were other churches, Rome and Alexandria in particular, which believed that John the Apostle resided in Asia.

We are also assured, this time on the evidence of an extract from Philip of Side (about 430), that Papias' work preserved reports of the Apostle's martyrdom in Palestine. The evidence must be regarded with caution. Eusebius of Caesarea, who was quite able to read, found nothing of the sort in the writings of Papias.[4]

According to tradition, in Asia as in Rome, the Fourth Gospel, composed at the end of the first century, was received as the work of John the Apostle. There seems to have been no objection, except on the part of a group of Christians in the second century, whom Epiphanius (who loved to multiply heresies) later made into the sect of the Alogi. The name is only a bad pun made up by Epiphanius himself.

The opposition possibly boils down to a single Roman priest, Caius.[5] This man's difficulties were of a rather special sort. He was a great adversary of the Montanists, who appealed to the Apocalypse. In order to cut at the roots of the evil he denied that the author of this book was the Apostle John. He extended his scruples to the Gospel, which he accused of being contradictory to the ordinary gospel of the Twelve, both in the way it relates the beginning of the public life and in the number of Passovers observed by Jesus during his ministry.

The late second-century document which we call the

---

[4] Cf. M.-J. Lagrange, *L'Évangile selon saint Jean* (Paris, 1925), pp. xxix–xlii

[5] This was the theory of Mgr Ladeuze. Cf. his article, 'Caius de Rome, le seul Aloge connu', in *Mélanges Godefroid Kurth* (Liège, 1908)

Muratorian Canon certainly appears to be answering the critical difficulties of the Alogi when it records tradition on the subject of the Fourth Gospel:

> The Fourth Gospel is that of John, one of the disciples. When his fellow-disciples and bishops urged him he said: 'Fast with me for three days from today, and we shall tell each other what has been revealed to us.' The same night it was revealed to Andrew, one of the Apostles, that John should write in his own name, with the sanction of them all. Consequently, though each book of the Gospels teaches the first facts in its own way, the faith of the believers finds no difference in them, since it is one sovereign Spirit who sets forth all things in each of them, about the Birth, the Passion, the Resurrection, the life with his disciples and his two-fold coming: in the first, despised, in the state of lowliness, but clothed with royal power and glorious in the second, which we still await. What wonder is it, then, if John states everything so boldly in his epistles, saying about him, 'That which we have seen with our eyes and heard with our ears, and our hands have handled—that is what we have written'? For in this manner he professes that he has not only seen and heard, but even written down all these marvellous deeds of the Lord, in their order.[6]

In fact, the Roman tradition is long prior to the Alogi. St Justin most probably reckoned this Gospel among the 'Memoirs of the Apostles'. The anti-Marcionite Prologue, a little after 150, asserts that it was published in John's lifetime, and appeals to the evidence of Papias.

In a passage of his *Hypotyposes*, preserved by Eusebius of Caesarea, Clement reveals both the interest which the Alexandrian church took in the Gospel of John and the secret of this special fondness: 'Seeing that the Gospels

[6] From the translation of M.-J. Lagrange, *Histoire ancienne du Canon du Nouveau Testament* (Paris, 1933), pp. 71 ff.

set forth only the material story, John, the last of all, entreated by his familiar friends and divinely upheld by the Spirit, wrote the *spiritual gospel*.'[7] Needless to relate, the Valentinian school at Alexandria had welcomed this Gospel enthusiastically, no doubt for its 'spiritual' character.

2

It is this character, stressed by Clement of Alexandria, which must help us to read and understand the Gospel of John. The 'spiritual gospel' will be the showing forth of the Word of God, who has revealed his glory by dwelling among us. As our guide to the deepest interpretation of the teaching and work of his Master we have an authorized witness, who was at the same time the beloved disciple and one who penetrated further than the others into the secrets of Jesus.

We must therefore read John's Gospel with his design in mind. That it is 'spiritual' means, for Clement of Alexandria, that it reveals the divine truths contained in the literal meaning; for the ancients in general it means that its doctrine has profound reverberations in the divine world and that his stories have a double significance: the one material, what actually happened: the other spiritual or allegorical, what the events—especially the miracles— symbolized, and all the mysterious teaching hidden in them. In other words, we must see the life of Christ as illuminated from within by the manifestation of the Word, who is Life and Light. The synoptics are chiefly concerned with the history; the Gospel of John is written on the historical plane, but in such a way that the historical plane receives the light projected from a higher plane, that of the manifestations of the Word.

[7] *H.E.*, VI, 14: 7

That is not all. This witness dissociates his evidence
from that of the Twelve. He refuses to be bound by the
traditional manner of presenting the gospel material.
Without any apparent benefit to his 'spiritual' thesis he
introduces new facts and even a new framework, remarkable at first sight for its multiplication of journeys to
Jerusalem. Luke's Gospel had already given us a hint
that the tradition of the Twelve represented only one
point of view, imposed on a much larger field of activity.
John's Gospel boldly breaks through the framework of
the synoptic tradition.

To help our comparisons, we found it useful to present
the arrangement of the first three Gospels in tabular form.
A similar form will help us to bring out the characteristics
of this Gospel, the originality of its framework and its
'spiritual' or allegorical tendency, superimposed on the
history. The division according to ideas is now mixed with
the historical and geographical divisions.

INTRODUCTION

(1) Theoretical prologue: the Logos, life and light
of men, is revealed in Jesus. Accessory idea:
John the Baptist was the witness who brought
men to the light (1: 1-18).

(2) The Baptist's witness (1: 19-34).

(3) How John's disciples (Andrew, Peter, Philip,
Nathanael) came to believe in Jesus as Messias
(1: 35-51).

FIRST PART: Jesus reveals himself.

I. (1) First revelation of Jesus' glory at *Cana*
(2: 1-11).

(2) Short stay of Jesus, his family and disciples, at
Capharnaum. The evangelist gives no details:
note the agreement with the synoptists (2: 12).

(3) Jesus goes up to Jerusalem for the *Passover*. The traders driven from the Temple. Episode of Nicodemus (2: 13–3: 21).

(4) In *Judaea*. Last witness of John the Baptist (3: 22–36).

(5) Returning to Galilee, Jesus passes through *Samaria*. Episode of the Samaritan woman. Evangelization of the Samaritans (4: 1–42).

II. (1) Return to *Galilee* (4: 43–45).

(2) At *Cana*. Second miracle at Cana: cure of the son of a royal official (*regulus*) from Capharnaum (4: 46–54).

(3) Jesus goes up to *Jerusalem* for *a feast*. Miracle at the Sheep-pool. Controversy with the Pharisees, and teachings in which Jesus reveals himself as Son of God (5: 1–47).

III. (1) *The other side of the Lake of Tiberias*. Multiplication of the loaves, shortly before the *Passover* (6: 1–15).

(2) *On the lake*: miracle (6: 16–21).

(3) *At Capharnaum*. Discourse on the bread of heaven, unbelief of the Jews, faith of the disciples (Judas Iscariot) (6: 22–71).

SECOND PART: Jesus rejected.

I. (1) Feast of the *Tabernacles* at Jerusalem. Teaching in the Temple. Violent opposition. Episode of the woman taken in adultery (7: 1–8: 11).

(2) Teaching and controversies (8: 12–59).

(3) Cure of the man born blind (9: 1–41).

(4) The Good Shepherd (10: 1–21).

(5) Feast of the *Dedication*. Discourse. Stoning (10: 22–39).

II. (1) In *Transjordan* (10: 40–42).

(2) Raising of Lazarus in *Bethany* (11: 1–53).

(3) Jesus at *Ephraim*. The *Passover* is near (11: 54–57).

(4) At *Bethany*. The anointing (12: 1–11).

(5) The entry into *Jerusalem*. Episode of the Greeks. Glorification by the voice from heaven. Unbelief of the Jews (12: 12–50).

THIRD PART: Jesus exalted.

I. (1) The washing of the feet and the Supper (13: 1–30).

(2) Consolation discourses; exhortations and predictions (13: 31–16: 33).

(3) The priestly prayer (17: 1–26).

II. (1) The Passion (18: 1–19: 42).

(2) The Resurrection (20: 1–31).

APPENDIX. Appearance on the lakeside. Peter and the beloved disciple (21: 1–25).

We are indeed far from the synoptic Gospels, but at the same time very close to them. Apart from the first two journeys to Jerusalem for the celebration of the first two Passovers, journeys which are inserted in the Galilean ministry, this Gospel's view of the public life remains perceptibly the same as that of the older traditional accounts: after a long period of evangelization in Galilee, Jerusalem becomes the chief theatre of Christ's activity, and that during the year before the final Passover. Even more striking is the resemblance with Luke's framework, which prolongs the last journey to Jerusalem.

There is also in this Gospel a moment, corresponding roughly to the synoptic arrangement, when Jesus' teaching separates him from the crowd and the Master has to reserve his secrets for his disciples (see the table, first part, III, (3)).

Within the Galilean section, just as in the common tradition, Capharnaum is in the foreground, as is the Lake of Tiberias: the chief novelty seems to be the interest shown in Cana of Galilee, which to some extent takes the place of Nazareth. That Christ should have moved about in the neighbourhood of Jerusalem in the last year of his life need not surprise us. That is the sort of divergence we must always expect whenever we encounter a fresh body of evidence. We recall that the 'gospel of the disciples' gave us some surprises over this section. Why should it be otherwise with the Gospel of the beloved disciple?

As for the facts, we find the same criss-cross of agreements and divergences. The three principal miracles, not recorded by the synoptics, are performed at Jerusalem (the paralysed man at the Sheep-pool, the man born blind, the raising of Lazarus). There is no room for them in the synoptic framework. John relates them because they so aptly illustrate the theme of his Gospel, that Jesus is Life and Light, and it was fitting that Jesus should show himself as Life and Light at Jerusalem. The other miracles, except that of Cana, are common to him and the synoptic tradition and besides, on this subject, St John has evidently meant to provide only some specially selected examples: the multiplication of the loaves, the miracle on the lake, the cure of the sick man of Capharnaum. The change of the water into wine at Cana is reported for its symbolic significance, and because it is the first of Jesus' 'signs'.

What most astonishes the critical reader is to note how different are the discourses in John's Gospel from the teaching according to the common tradition. On the one hand, in the oral style, we have a programme for the reform of morals, as preparation for the Kingdom; on the other, we have the revealing of Jesus' relations with his Father and the communication to men of the privileges of his divinity (knowledge of God's secrets, divine life, glory); and all this in a style appropriate to the subject, solemn and hieratic.

Is it possible that the teacher who delivered the Sermon on the Mount was also the 'revealer' come down from heaven to tell us the secrets of God and make us partakers in them?

If Jesus is the teacher of religion, invested with divine authority, as the synoptic Gospels themselves reveal him, if he is the Son of God in very truth and could speak to men about his Father and about heaven, it must be admitted that he would express himself in the manner and style of the Fourth Gospel. Already, when the Christ of the synoptic tradition reveals the Father (Mt. 11: 25–30; Lk. 10: 21–22), he speaks in no other wise. Even in the synoptics he very often puts forward his own person, demanding for himself the love due to God alone. A revelation can but suggest the world beyond and repeat itself indefinitely in suggesting it, whence arises the monotony of the formulas of some discourses. Whence, too, perhaps, a greater freedom to be allowed to the reporter. The memory could not be assisted as it was in the oral style.

Fr Lagrange rightly compares the discourses of the Fourth Gospel and their dialogues with some pages of Jeremias: 'They have no parallel,' he writes, 'except in the preaching of the Israelite prophets, and specially in that of Jeremias, so often contradicted, threatened, beaten, put in prison, and finally made the victim of his own zeal for the religious and temporal interests of his people. . . . All we know of the life of Jeremias is hardly more than the reception given to his words, which were spoken in the name of God.[8] There are passages, too, in the Wisdom literature, where Wisdom speaks in the first person, which reveal features in common with the Johannine style.

The beloved disciple appears, then, to be on a different plane to that of the Twelve. He was a 'witness' of a special kind. Peter and the Twelve had remembered chiefly what had happened in Galilee and the teaching Jesus had given to the crowds whom he was preparing for the Kingdom of God. The disciple observed rather the events in Jerusalem, Jesus' confidences to the Twelve and those teachings in which, driven to extremity by the ill will of the Pharisees, he disclosed who he was. He had meditated on the deep sayings uttered by Jesus, which he had not always fully understood at the time; he had understood them better later on, in the light cast by the Holy Spirit on the life of the Church. As a witness he recorded for us the words of Jesus; as an inspired theologian he interpreted them. Is not the disciple's interpretation likely to fall short of the Master's thought rather than to go beyond it? He also understood the intentions with which Jesus had wrought some of his miraculous deeds. When he opened the eyes of the man born blind, was he not thinking of the religious blindness of the men of his generation? The illuminating energy of the divine Word was symbolized in his miraculous power. When he raised Lazarus from the dead, he was teaching that he is the life of souls and that those who believe in him never die. That is what the beloved disciple understood when he became, in the Holy Spirit, the seer of the full realities. In the beginning, perhaps, he did not exhaust the full significance of the drama at which he had been present. Later on he was its inspired expositor.

[8] *Évangile selon saint Jean*, p. lxxxviii

To a lesser degree, St Luke's Gospel too diverged from the common tradition. The Seventy-two remembered some things which the Twelve had passed over in silence. A new scene, Samaria, was shown to us, and here we may note the relationship with John's Gospel. New characters come on the scene, and here too we can be sure there are many hidden harmonies between his memoirs and those of John. I need only allude to the family at Bethany.

3

It is with good cause that tradition has given John the title of 'theologian'. Our Fourth Gospel is the authoritative witness to the revelation contained in the message of Jesus.

The prologue to the Gospel is a theological composition. In our day, criticism sees in it the form proper to liturgical hymns. It matters little if John has imitated or even appropriated a hymn to Christ the Word: the thought of the prologue is all his own, and his vision is that of the Eagle.

> In the beginning was the Word,
> and the Word was with God,
> and the Word was God. . . .
>
> All things were made through him
> and without him was made nothing that hath
>   been made.
>
> In him was life,
> and the life was the light of men. . . .
>
> He was in the world
> and the world was made through him,
> and the world knew him not.

He came to what was his,
and his own received him not.

But to as many as received him
he gave power to become children of God,
to them that believed in his Name.

The great theological novelty, the great affirmation, is that Christ is the Logos, the Word. But St Paul, the other great interpreter of the theological significance of Christ's work, he too calls Christ the image of God, the first-born of all creation, him through whom all things were created. The Son of God of the synoptic Gospels, as they represent him, possessed a transcendent personality which could easily be identified with the hypostasis (the Wisdom of God, the divine Word) foreshadowed by the Old Testament. It is false to suppose that there was an abrupt incursion into the New Testament, through St John, of a philosophical notion from Hellenism. The theology of the Word has its roots in the Old Testament and it expresses the most authentic Christian thought.

St John then will have us see the Word, the Son of God made man, dwelling among us, revealing his glory. To obtain this result he claims to put before us merely the evidence of what he has seen. The Gospel itself must be theological. But how can we show that St John was able to turn the gospel message into theology without destroying its nature as a gospel?

His art lies in this, that he has chosen and isolated just those elements, already contained in the authentic message of Jesus, which had not received from the synoptics all the emphasis that he gives them. It is not difficult to find formulas in the first three Gospels corresponding to those in John. But there they are usually set in a context which does not at once enable us to grasp them in all their theological import. John stresses them by isolating them; their elements take on a new significance; we understand them in a new light. This is not to falsify the historical perspective, because the evangelist warns us of his aim and because his teaching, so far from suppressing the message of the common tradition, is based upon it, while adding to it other memories. A few examples will suffice.

The discourses in the Gospel establish the great revelation that Jesus is the Word. Never would John place this expression on the lips of Christ. Jesus speaks of his relations with the Father, as he does in the ordinary tradition, but he puts more stress on them. The stress is John's, but the doctrine is that of the common tradition. Similarly the formulas of Light and Life have analogies in the synoptic tradition. The revelations about the Holy Spirit were already contained in the promise Jesus made to his Apostles, when sending them out to preach, that the Holy Spirit would speak in them (Mt. 10: 20), but John has emphasized them.

In the realm of eschatology also the Fourth Gospel is strongly contrasted with the synoptics. The Christ of the common tradition, we are sometimes told, preaches the Kingdom of Heaven; the Johannine Christ substitutes for this message the *mystique* of an eternal life already present on earth in those who believe in Jesus. The supposed contrast arises once again from the fact that St John isolates one element of the common doctrine. The Kingdom of God, as we have noted in passing, already begins on earth, in the Church (that is, St Matthew's gospel) and in the presence of the Holy Spirit (the gospel of St Luke). Is it so far from these anticipations to that of St John? It is an accepted rule that the messianic and eschatological gifts come down from heaven and begin in this world: for the whole of primitive Christianity the coming of Christ marks a breaking-in to this world of the world beyond. According to the synoptics, Christ taught that those who accepted his message received into themselves the seeds of a new life, the life of children of the Kingdom. Once again the teaching of John isolates and defines. On the other hand, eschatology is found in the Fourth Gospel. Jesus rarely speaks in it of the Kingdom of God: that is true. He more often speaks of *the life eternal*, which is an equivalent for it: he foretells his resurrection and the coming of the Holy Spirit.

One of the central ideas of this Gospel is the unity of the disciples with each other and with God through Christ. Is this a novelty of John's? We have but to read the saying from St Luke's Gospel: 'Fear not, little flock, for it has pleased your Father to give you a Kingdom.' We cannot give these words their full value without arriving at St John's phrase: 'I am the Good Shepherd.'

John makes it clear that the unity of Christians with each other is a unity of life; in this sense he goes beyond the synoptics' doctrine. But that is not to say that he substitutes his thought for that of Christ. The knowledge of God which our Lord gives us, his revelation, is a living religion, faith and love as well as knowledge; St John has not falsified Christianity on this point. But faith and love imply that life is communicated. The Johannine notion of the Church, with its unity derived from the life of the Vine-trunk, expresses the thought of Christ. It corresponds to the idea of the Kingdom of God, to the 'mystical' idea of a divine reality in the order of intellect (revelation) and in the order of life, which penetrates the institution. This may seem to link up with Greek mysticism, but it could be maintained with as much or with more reason that it is a way of representing what is familiar to religious souls. St John had his reasons for attributing it to Jesus.

Without neglecting the factual details or historical truth, St John shows us Jesus, the Son of God, revealing himself to the world; he ignores the educational work of progressive revelation, which is made plain in the earlier Gospels. He has no thought of substituting his point of view for that of his predecessors. His is something else, a light from above which falls on the human events in order to show up, from the beginning, their full significance.

Finally, the Apostle accentuates the points in Jesus' doctrine which specially interested Christianity at the end of the first century. His Gospel stands up against Judaism and various tendencies which threatened the purity of the Church's faith. Against Judaism it was enough to bring out the real opposition which Jesus had encountered. Against the sect of the Baptist, which had developed alongside Christianity, he indicated its refutation even in the prologue. Lastly and chiefly, against those tendencies to intellectualist Gnosticism which betrayed the specific character of the Christian revelation, the religion of the Fourth Gospel gives faith and charity their due place. He insists on our Lord's manhood against those very widespread tendencies which wanted to see in Christ a purely divine being and left him only the shadow of a human nature: the Johannine Christ is incarnate in the full sense. He is the Man who wearied himself searching for us and died in pain on the Cross.

4

As was only to be expected, criticism has been very active over the Fourth Gospel. For those who do not admit simply that it is an apostolic witness, the great enigma must be to explain its duality: that it is theological, yet preserves such indubitable contact with the primitive tradition. These critics were bound to yield to the temptation to divide up the theology and the historical data between several authors, nor have they failed to do so. These attempts are described at length in New Testament commentaries and introductions.

Then followed studies devoted to placing this Gospel in a new and wider religious background. It has been related to Platonic philosophy, or to Hellenistic Judaism (Philo of Alexandria). At the moment there is a preference for Gnosticism: the world of the Hermetic and Mandaean cults is being explored.[9] The inevitable reaction has set in. The Aramaic basis of the Gospel has been brought to light:[10] stress is being laid on its double aspect, both Jewish and Hellenistic. From the manuscripts recently discovered in the caves of the Judaean desert (the Dead Sea scrolls) we may hazard the guess that Jewish sects contemporary with Christianity may have spoken a religious language which had affinities with that of St John.

The days are past when the Johannine enigma could be resolved by fantastic solutions. The Gospel of John was in existence at the beginning of the second century, and from then on it was ascribed to John the Apostle, the son of Zebedee. One need no longer have recourse to Hellenism to explain the idea that the deepest religious truths were revealed by the incarnate Son of God.

[9] The great commentary of R. Bultmann (Göttingen, 1941) makes a synthesis of all these critical works. In the version of the evangelist it distinguishes a narrative source deriving from the synoptics and the revelation discourses, with which it looks for parallels in later Gnosticism (*Odes of Solomon*, etc.).

[10] Bibliography in Lagrange, *op. cit.*, pp. ci–ciii

CHAPTER SIX

The Tetramorphic Gospel

FOR a fairly long period, extending into the second century, the oral tradition existed side by side with the written Gospels. When we have analysed this state of affairs we shall return to our written Gospels and see how the four received the position due to them, as the Church became clearly conscious of the part henceforth to be played by Scripture in ensuring the fidelity of the apostolic witness.

I

As long as the Apostles and their immediate disciples were alive, the Christian communities had recourse to the oral tradition. It was in fact the living voice of Christ which had formed the souls of the first disciples. It was that which conveyed the power of God; it was by reproducing the living voice of the message of Jesus that the Apostles had founded the churches. 'The gospel', said St Paul in his letter to the Romans, 'is the power of God, bringing salvation to every one that believeth.'[1]

All the Apostles endorsed this profoundly true saying of the convert of Damascus. But still, they and their immediate disciples died; the authorized voices were silent. During the second century several generations of 'Elders' devoutly preserved the memories of the apostolic age. Papias and Polycarp still trusted to have access by this means to the authentic teachings of Christ.

[1] Rom. 1: 16

To be quite frank, the traditions which were being handed on from mouth to mouth were already, in the second century, drifting into troubled waters. The Elders consulted by Papias were repeating sayings like this: 'The days will come when vines shall spring up, each having ten thousand stems, and each stem will have ten thousand branches, and each branch ten thousand twigs. Each twig will have ten thousand clusters, and each cluster ten thousand grapes, and a single grape will yield twenty-five measures of wine . . . and so with wheat and other crops. . . .'[2]

For the oral tradition to be preserved in its integrity, it had to be effectively protected by God. God does not work unnecessary miracles. Following a design of Providence, the Apostles (or, with their approval, their disciples) set down in writing the essentials of the oral tradition.

The Gnostics for their part wilfully hung back. When it was clear to all that the voice of the oral gospel, according to the communal, public tradition, was extinct, they fell back on alleged traditions, secretly handed down, claiming that these were more trustworthy than the common teachings for the vulgar. In the next chapter we shall make the acquaintance of an apocryphal gospel literature which arose in Gnostic circles.

Even Clement of Alexandria had not quite abandoned the dream of getting at the apostolic, oral tradition apart from the public teaching of the Gospels. But he did not, like Papias or Polycarp, expect information on the life or doctrine of Jesus which is not found in the written Gospels. Following in this point the tendency of the Alexandrian church as revealed by Pseudo-Barnabas and heretical Gnosticism, he believed he could

[2] Fragm. I, 2

come at a tradition of *gnosis*. 'After his resurrection,'
he wrote in his *Hypotyposes*, 'the Lord imparted the
knowledge [*gnosis*] to James the Just, to John and Peter;
these delivered it to the rest of the Apostles, and they
to the seventy, of whom Barnabas was one.'[3] Clement
believed himself to be the heir of this gnosis through the
channel of the Elders.[4] In his system, it is very probably
no more than a profounder way of penetrating the
common teaching and of understanding the hidden
allegories of the gospel.

St Irenaeus clearly sees the situation and adopts the
position it requires. He rejects the distinction between the
common teaching and the gnosis and moreover does not
admit the existence of secret traditions. For him, the
voice of the Apostles is normally expressed in the written
Gospels. The function of tradition, perpetuated in the
teaching of the Elders and the bishops of the apostolic
churches, is to keep the faith intact; as regards the
Gospels, it is to preserve the purity of their text and their
sound interpretation, and at the same time to guarantee
their apostolic origin.

2

In fact then, in the nature of things, the voice of the
oral tradition was silenced fairly soon. The written
Gospels took its place in their own way, but of course the
apostolic tradition continued to live alongside the written
Gospels and to play the part so well defined by St
Irenaeus.

The liturgy shows that the change-over had taken place
by the middle of the second century. St Justin is the first

---

[3] Eusebius, *H.E.*, II, 1, 4; cf. G. Bardy, *La Théologie de l'Église de
saint Clément de Rome à saint Irénée*, p. 176
[4] Cf. G. Bardy, *ibid.*, pp. 175–177

to tell us of the reading of the Gospels at the celebration of the Supper. 'On the day which is called the Sun's day, all (of our people) who live in the towns or the country meet in one place and the Memoirs of the Apostles or the writings of the prophets are read, as much as time permits. When the reader has finished, the president says some words of admonition and exhorts us to imitate these excellent examples.'[5] The written Gospels, these 'Memoirs of the Apostles', are now among the springs which water the Christian life.

Because Harnack did not understand how the predominance of the spoken word over the written was automatically reversed, he imagined that it was their promotion to liturgical use on a level with the prophets which caused our Gospels to be given the character of canonical and inspired books. This theory precisely reverses the order of values.

When Papias searched for the 'living and permanent voice', it was in order to hear the voice of the divine Logos who speaks to us in the new revelation: 'God, having spoken of old to the fathers through the prophets by many partial revelations and in various ways, in these last days hath spoken to us by one who is Son.'[6]

This divine speech of the Son, of which the Gospel, even in its written form, was still the expression, could not on any account be subordinated to the prophets, as Harnack would have it. For all Christians Christ was 'the Sceptre of the divine Majesty',[7] the expression of God's power; his word, like his action, had displayed this power to the world. Word and action had continued to be effective in the sacred speech of the Gospels. In the eyes

[5] *Apol.*, I, 65
[6] Heb. 1: 1–2
[7] 1 Clem., 16, 2

of Christians, the prophets received their own authority from Christ. In the thought of St Ignatius of Antioch, for example, they owe their position to the fact that they were promulgators, by anticipation, of the Gospel, and by their lives were disciples of Christ.[8]

St Justin believes the same:

Just as Abraham believed the voice of God, and this was reckoned to him for justice, so we, believing the voice of God, which has sounded out anew through the Apostles of Christ, and has been preached to us by the prophets, renounce all that is of the world, even unto death.[9]

All the second-century texts must be given their true sense. This voice of God, which sounds out through the Apostles, is the gospel: what the prophets preached, what gave them authority, was the gospel, even then.

For Christians, the revelation of the Word of God, made concrete in the oral teaching of the Apostles and then in the written Gospels, was from the outset the sole rule of life, the truth superior to all others. There could only be one Master, Christ; there existed only one true prophet, to whom all others must be referred—the Christ, the divine Word.

The moment when the written gospel replaces the oral tradition is also the moment when the dignity and divinity of Christ are most clearly expressed in his title of Logos, the Word of God. It may be that the sense of 'living Speech', with which the term *Verbum* was invested, was attenuated later, during the Christological controversies. In the second century the word distinctly implies the idea of God's manifestation through speech. The Christian's faith is expressed in the words of St Ignatius of Antioch:

[8] *Magn.*, 8, 2
[9] *Dial.* 119

One only God, who manifested himself through Jesus Christ his Son, who is his Word, coming forth from silence, who in all things pleased him who sent him.[10]

The 'Word', who spoke in his teaching, in his miracles, in his example, in his death and in his resurrection—the gospel we read is that very speech still resounding in our midst. The superiority of Christianity over the message of John the Baptist and over the prophets lies precisely in this, that it actually hears this speech. The Gnostic Heracleon explains somewhere that John the Baptist was only the *voice*, which did not yet distinctly pronounce the speech, but still is nearer than its echo; the prophets, however, were only the 'echo'; they gave men a presentiment of the Speech which would resound one day. . . .[11]

In view of all this, how could the Gospels have needed to be placed on the footing of the prophets in order to receive the rank of the divine Speech?

3

We can now easily understand the significance attached by the second-century Church to the written Gospels, or rather to the one and only Gospel which is transmitted to us through apostolic authority. The written gospel remains the speech of Christ, that which God spoke to us through the voice and the whole life of Christ. Because it reveals God, it is invested with his power, and among men it is the supremely effectual force which triumphs over error and establishes the Kingdom of God. The Gospel was preached by the Apostles, then written by them or endued with their authority, promulgated and written in the Spirit of God: the Apostles were the manifold voices of one sole prophecy, far superior in authority

[10] *Magn.*, 8, 2
[11] Fragm. 5 (ed. W. Völker, p. 65)

and dignity to that of the Old Testament prophets, for these were only its echo and preparation.

In a moment we shall hear St Irenaeus summing up in deathless words this faith of the whole Church. A preliminary reflection will help us to grasp it better.

Towards the middle of the second century there was a moment of synthesis, when the Church became clearly and decisively aware of its own treasure: aware that in its four Gospels it possessed the 'Memoirs of the Apostles' (the expression is St Justin's) and that nothing could ever be added to them. From that moment the four Gospels formed an indivisible whole, one unique Gospel, in four editions, 'according to' Matthew, John, Mark or Luke. Irenaeus, Clement of Alexandria and the Muratorian Canon already use this last expression, which perfectly states the ideal unity of the gospel. The word used by St Irenaeus, the 'tetramorphic' gospel (in four forms or manners of presentation) is expressive, and we have therefore chosen it as the title of this chapter.[12]

In a later chapter we shall see that the sects which cut themselves off from the Church only left it when they had abandoned the greater part of the common treasure or replaced the pure gold of tradition with man-made tinsel, but even so, in their very defection, they took with them *a gospel*. Basilides, Marcion and the Judaeo-Christians before them limited the gospel and adulterated it: none of them could do without it.

The Great Church, on the contrary, kept the whole treasure. Every local church was made rich with the treasure which belonged to all. Matthew had written for the faithful of Palestine; Mark in Peter's name and Luke

---

[12] The word is possible in English and not inappropriate. In Christian art, a tetramorph is 'the union of the attributes of the four evangelists in one winged figure' (Concise Oxford Dictionary). (*Translator*)

in Paul's, for those of Rome; John for the Christian communities of Asia. But as the Church was conscious of being one, of forming only one people, so each Apostle spoke for the Christians of the whole world; Paul or Peter, John or Matthew, they were the heralds of the sole Teacher. These four apart, no Apostle had published a written gospel. No other apostolic authority was given to a gospel. The false claims of sects separated from the Church could not give authority to the so-called gospels of Matthew or Peter or the Twelve Apostles.[13]

Before 150 the Church in Rome, meeting-place of all truths as of all errors, knew quite clearly what to hold fast and imposed her faith, or rather the faith of all, on all the churches.

Irenaeus, who uses the expression 'tetramorphic gospel', is therefore no innovator. He is evidently working on the common faith, and this is so firmly anchored and so venerable that he can already afford to find mystical reasons for this number of 'four', which is henceforth inseparable from the apostolic promulgation of the gospel. He writes:

We do not know the plan of our salvation through any others than those through whom the gospel came to us; that which they then preached they later handed on to us, by the will of God, in the Scriptures, to be the foundation and the pillar of our faith. . . . They went out through the whole world, proclaiming to men the peace of heaven, each and all of them possessing the gospel of God. Thus Matthew both preached the gospel and set it in writing among the Hebrews, in their own language, while Peter and Paul were evangelizing in Rome, and founding the Church. After their departure Mark too,

[13] Cf. G. Bardy, *La Théologie de l'Église de saint Clément de Rome à saint Irénée*, p. 189

the disciple and interpreter of Peter, gives us Peter's preaching in writing. Then Luke, Paul's companion, wrote in a book the gospel he had preached. Last of all, John, the disciple of the Lord, who had lain on his breast, he too wrote a Gospel, while he lived at Ephesus in Asia.[14]

Such is the very rigid line to which (since it concerns the faith) the history is reduced. But the history, as we have tried to reconstruct it in rather greater complexity, could hardly be better summarized than in this line.

And now comes the mystical interpretation, which presumes, as we have said, that the truth of the history has long been taken for granted.

There are four regions of the inhabited world, and four principal winds, and the Church is spread over the whole earth; and the pillar and ground of the Church is the Gospel and the Spirit of Life: therefore it is natural that there should be four pillars, everywhere breathing out incorruption and giving life to men. From this it is clear that the Logos, who has created all things, who is seated on the cherubim and contains all things, in revealing himself to men has given us the tetramorphic gospel, upheld by one only Spirit. . . . And indeed the cherubim are shown under four aspects, which are symbols of the activity of the Son of God. 'The first living creature is like a lion',[15] thus showing his vigorous, governing and royal character; 'the second is like an ox', indicating his connexion with the sacrifice and the priestly order; 'the third has the face of a man', thus clearly showing his coming in a human nature; 'the fourth is like a flying eagle', indicating the gift of the Spirit who comes to hover over the Church. The Gospels are therefore to be compared with the creatures on whom Christ is seated.

[14] *Adv. Haer.*, III, 1, 1
[15] Irenaeus quotes Apoc. 4: 7, reproducing Ezechiel.

Irenaeus then explains that the Gospel of John corresponds to the lion (the generation of the Word is the source of his power), the Gospel of Luke to the ox (it begins with Zachary's sacrifice), and that of Matthew to the man (because of the genealogy); the Gospel of Mark has the eagle for its symbol, for it begins with the prophecy of Isaias, and the prophets surveyed the future with the soaring range of an eagle.[16] He concludes:

> This being the case, they are foolish, senseless and above all presumptuous, who destroy the essence of the gospel and either increase or lessen the number of the 'forms' of the gospel: the former, to make us think they have found more truth, the latter, to destroy the work of God.[17]

Origen was to find other mystical meanings. Our Lord's Apostles dig the wells in the desert, which are stopped up with earth and filth by the Jews' slowness of understanding;[18] they blow the priestly trumpets which overthrew Jericho:

> Our Lord Jesus Christ, at his coming, sends the priests, his Apostles, holding trumpets of bronze, the glorious and heavenly doctrine of his preaching. Matthew, the first, in his Gospel blew the priestly trumpet: Mark too, Luke and John, made each one his priestly trumpet to resound.[19]

Now let us hear the Church's faith translated into juridical language. As an African and a jurist, Tertullian accentuates the legal character of the gospel, by borrowing from legal language the word *instrumentum*, meaning a 'juridical act' or 'title':

[16] St Jerome and St Augustine gave the symbolism its classic form, in which Mark has the symbol of the lion and John that of the eagle.

[17] *Adv. Haer.*, III, 11, 8

[18] *Hom. in Gen.*, XIII, 1–2

[19] *Hom. in Jesu Nave*, VII, 1

In the first place we establish that the Gospels' 'title' has for its 'guarantor' the Apostles, to whom the Lord gave this charge of promulgating the gospel, and also apostolic men, not alone, but in union with the Apostles.

Thus all our texts evince the peaceable possession of truth. The truth is pointed indeed against the heresies. But that is not to say that the Church has imitated Marcion, and that he, the heretic, who eliminated the Old Testament in favour of the New, was the first to confer the dignity of canonical books on the New Testament writings!

From the very beginning, as we said, the Church ranked the revelation of the Word of God above the prophets, that is, the Old Testament. Against Marcion and the Alexandrian Gnostics she had to maintain the real though subordinate value of the old prophets. So far from saying that she invested the New Testament with the dignity of the Old, we must state that, while keeping an exact proportion and remembering the preparatory function of the Old Testament revelation, she would not agree to deprive the latter of the dignity it derived from the inspiration of the Spirit; she insisted that the Spirit had spoken because of Christ, had spoken about Christ and had spoken as already representing the divine Logos, but she maintained that he did speak in the ancient books.

The truth is that the Church—the Roman Church more than all—strong in her faith and in the tradition of all the churches, firmly resisted all formulas which would diminish or distort the truth of the tetramorphic gospel.

We shall have occasion in the next chapter to speak of the gospels fabricated by the heretics. The Church ruthlessly rejected them. She took the disciples of Valentinus to task, when they set St John's Gospel on a pinnacle, just because it could be more easily accommodated to their doctrine. She reproached Marcion (about 145) for having set his heart on the Gospel of Luke alone and for having cut it about and arranged it to suit himself. She vigorously opposed the Montanists, who eagerly ranked the 'oracles' of their prophets with those of the Old and New Testaments, as if these gave the Church a new 'title', a revelation to make good the incomplete or obscure revelation of the two Testaments (we know that this was to prove a temptation to all subsequent 'spirituals', especially the Abbot Joachim of Flora). She was equally opposed to the enemies of the Montanists, when they dared to strike the Johannine scriptures out of the Canon, on the pretext that they favoured the visions of the 'spirituals'.

The controversies of the Roman church were therefore the occasion of defining the received traditions about the origin of our Gospels. A little after the year 150 a Catholic edition of the four Gospels was published in Rome. It was a reply to the gospel of Marcion. On the occasion of this publication, a member of the Roman church composed short prologues to each of the Gospels. That to Matthew is lost. The others have been preserved, that to St Luke being in Greek. We mentioned it earlier, in connexion with all the Gospels.[20]

It seems likely that a document of the end of the second century, which we usually call the Muratorian Canon (after Muratori, the scholar who discovered it at Milan and published it in 1740), indicates the faith of the Roman church and also her disapproval of the position of the Alogi. That is a reason for attributing its authorship to St Hippolytus. Its tone well fits the temperament

[20] D. De Bruyne, 'Les plus Anciens Prologues Latins des Évangiles', in *Revue Bénédictine*, vol. XL (1928), pp. 193–214

of that enigmatic personality, who defended the true faith with authority and iron resolution, especially against the Gnostics, and who wrote against Caius the Alogus.

We reproduce the beginning of the Canon—preserved in a wretched Latin translation—according to Fr Lagrange's attempt at restoration. The first lines are lost. They were no doubt about the tetramorphic gospel, then about Matthew. Then followed the prefaces to Mark, Luke and John, the last of which has been quoted earlier.

(Mark followed the preachings of Peter, those) at least at which he was present, and wrote according to that.

Thirdly, the book of the Gospel of St. Luke. This Luke was a physician. After the Ascension of Christ, Paul took him as assistant, because of his knowledge of law; with his consent he wrote what he judged right.

But he too never saw the Lord in the flesh. And in consequence, as far as he could ascertain (the story), he began to tell it, starting from the birth of John.

The fourth Gospel is that of John, one of the disciples. When his fellow-disciples and bishops urged him, he said: 'Fast with me for three days from today, and we shall tell each other what has been revealed to us.' The same night it was revealed to Andrew, one of the Apostles, that John should write in his own name, with the sanction of them all. Consequently, though each book of the Gospels tells the first facts in its own way, the faith of the believers finds no difference in them, since it is one sovereign Spirit who sets forth all things in each of them, about the Birth, the Passion, the Resurrection, the life with his disciples and his two-fold coming; in the first, despised, in the state of lowliness, but clothed with royal power and glorious in the second, which we still await. What wonder is it, then, if John states everything so boldly in his epistles, saying about him: 'That which we have seen with our eyes and heard with our ears, and our hands have handled—that is what we have written'? For in this manner he professes that he has not only seen and also heard, but even written down all these marvellous deeds of the Lord, in their order. . . .

4

The Muratorian Canon provides the complete list of the New Testament books. From the end of the first century, the Epistles of St Paul had been collected in one *corpus*. The four Gospels naturally formed a unity. The various writings of John, Luke and Peter were as naturally grouped together.

A greater precision in doctrine appears when all these writings in their turn are grouped in a higher unity, and together constitute the 'New Testament', henceforth distinguished from the Old. This innovation—it is so only in the sense that Christians became aware of what was already present in their thought—adds nothing to the dignity of the Gospels. They remain the 'Speech' (the manifestation of the Word) and inspired expression of the apostolic witness. They gain nothing in dignity by being placed alongside the inspired books of the Old Testament. But it means that more attention is paid to the authority and sacred character of the *books*. From now on, the written Gospels, *as such*, will be accorded honour in the liturgy, copied even more devotedly than before, respected in the letter and commented on as sacred books. The Church was born of the gospel; henceforth she is aware of her rights and duties; she extends her care to the guardianship of her books, she claims the duty and the right to interpret them in the light of the Holy Spirit ever abiding with her.

The originals and earliest copies of our Gospels were perhaps written on papyrus rolls. But from the second century, in Christian practice, the roll was often replaced by the papyrus 'codex', which was easier to handle when the writing was of some length and had to be handled frequently. It seems that from the beginning Christians showed a preference for the codex, a more popular form than the roll, and in fact the oldest fragment we possess of a manuscript of St John's Gospel, going back to the first half of the second century, is a fragment of codex. So is the Bodmer papyrus, of the same Gospel (end of the second century). The remains of the 'unknown gospel' of the same period (which we shall mention later) are also written on codex leaves. The Christian literary papyri of the second and third centuries originate almost entirely from codices. Our oldest manuscript of the four Gospels (the Chester Beatty papyrus, of the first half of the third century) is a codex, in which the order seems to have been Matthew, John, Luke, Mark. As a rule, then, the tetramorphic gospel was presented in this way.

One of Justin's disciples, Tatian 'the Assyrian', composed for his compatriots of the Adiabene (the region of Mosul) and the land of Edessa (or Urfa) a gospel which combined the four canonical Gospels in one single text. For two centuries it was the gospel of the Syrians. Aphraates and St Ephrem made commentaries on it. The tetramorphic gospel had thus become the *Diatessaron*, the 'four Gospels in one'. Tatian's work, which had no lasting success except in the Syriac-speaking church of Syria, was first composed in Greek.

The Doura-Europos excavations have recently recovered for us a fragment of the Greek *Diatessaron*. A tiny square of parchment, all that is left of a liturgical roll buried in the glacis of the Doura ramparts between 254 and 256–7, gives us fourteen short lines of this first 'gospel harmony'; the end of the episode of the Galilean women witnessing Christ's agony, and the beginning of the story of the burial. It is an artificial mosaic of the gospel texts, constructed with a scholar's art. We give a translation of it, with the references in brackets.

... of Zebedee (Mt. 27: 56) and Salome (Mk. 15: 40) and the wives of those who had followed him from Galilee, watching the Crucified (Lk. 23: 49).

It was the day of the Preparation, and the Sabbath began to dawn (Lk. 23: 54). Evening having fallen on the Preparation, that is, the eve of the sabbath (Mk. 15: 42), there came a man (Mt. 27: 57), who was a member of the Council (Lk. 23: 50), of Arimathaea, a town of Judaea (Lk. 23: 51), called Joseph (Mt. 27: 57), a good man and just (Lk. 23: 50), a disciple of Jesus, but secretly for fear of the Jews (Jn. 19: 38); and he, too, was looking for the kingdom of God (Lk. 23: 51). He had not consented to their resolution (Lk. 23: 51).

Into the general plan provided by St. Luke's Gospel Tatian works in the details of the other evangelists, without losing a piece. At the same time the story comes to life. A scarcely perceptible stroke, here and there, ensures the vigour of the style. The episode of the women of Galilee had ended baldly, 'watching these things'. Tatian writes 'watching the Crucified', and the pathos of the scene is felt.

Fr Lagrange gives a masterly analysis of this episode of Joseph of Arimathaea:

Once again we must pay homage to the extreme skill of the harmonist. For this very short introduction to the intervention of Joseph of Arimathaea, he has drawn mainly on Luke, but he allots an important part to Mark, he has not neglected John and finally he has taken two sayings from Matthew. With these *membra disjecta* he has composed a narrative in which everything follows in logical order, yet the interest is maintained; the setting of the time; a man comes forward; he is a senator, representing a town which is at once named. His name is put in the centre, then his natural qualities. He was Jesus' disciple, but in secret; he was waiting for the kingdom of God and had not been a party to the design of condemning Jesus. This order is better than that of Luke, who inserts Joseph's origin in a rather awkward parenthesis.[21]

In the nature of the case, Tatian had to solve the many problems raised by the harmonization of the different gospel stories. We already know that one problem was the duration of Jesus' life. He fits the Gospel of John to the synoptics' pattern and thus reduces the public ministry to a year and some months. As we do again today, he followed John for the events of the opening of the public life: the calls of Andrew and the unknown disciple, then of Peter, Philip and Nathanael, and the wedding at Cana. Then he rejoined Luke for the stay at Nazareth. He allowed only one expulsion of the traders from the Temple and for this followed the chronology of the synoptics. The choice of the Apostles took place on the mountain, whence Jesus came down to the plain and preached the discourse which is common to Matthew and Luke.

But we know it well enough: a harmony inevitably sacrifices the peculiar character of each Gospel. Our Gospels were not made to be harmonized. Each of them draws an authentic portrait of Jesus. To mix their traits is to introduce into the divine work an element of human thought, a choice which cannot but be personal and arbitrary; and in any case, in proportion as one refrains from making it a personal work—and Tatian hardly

[21] *Critique textuelle*, II (Paris, 1935), p. 630

attempts this—it is to substitute a blurred image for the four incomparable portraits.

Other attempts in later ages at harmonies in Greek and in Latin proved abortive. Tatian's work itself, after enjoying a great success in the Syrian church, was eliminated in the fifth century, at least from liturgical use. It was only right, not so much because this work was suspected of heresy, as because it sacrificed the individual character of the 'Four'. We can readily endorse the canon which Rabbula, bishop of Edessa from 411 to 435, decreed for his church: 'Let the priests and deacons have care that in all the churches there be a "gospel of the distinct [sc. evangelists]", and that it be read.' The Tetramorph, in fact, not the *Diatessaron*.

CHAPTER SEVEN

On the Fringes of the Four

T HIS chapter is devoted to some phenomena which are wholly or partly accounted for by the genuine survival of the oral tradition, or at least by belief in it: apocryphal gospels, notable variants of the gospel manuscripts and quotations of our Lord's sayings which are not found in the canonical Gospels. In all this there is far more chaff than good grain, but it is not impossible that a grain or two of the divine words may be discovered.

I

The second century witnessed a luxuriant growth of the gospels, now called 'apocryphal' to distinguish them from the canonical literature. Some were composed within the Church; the majority saw the light in heretical sects, which took advantage of the prevailing climate of opinion to propagate their errors under the guise of tradition. There had also to be replies to new kinds of curiosity, not satisfied by the canonical Gospels; many were eager to learn more about Jesus' kinsfolk or the blessed Virgin, or to know the minutest details about such essential facts as the Resurrection.

Let us take a rapid glance at this gospel literature. It is not impossible that in some cases it may have preserved some good traditions. But, as we shall see, the chances of this are very slight. Generally it is either inspired by the canonical Gospels or it is pure invention or it embroiders some fragments of historical truth. But at least it will show us, by contrast, the value of the authentic 'Memoirs'.

The gospel of the Judaeo-Christians, which goes back to the first century, must be considered by itself. We ought really to speak of several gospels: the 'Gospel according to the Hebrews', the 'Gospel of the Ebionites', the 'Gospel of the Nazarenes'. The question is so complicated, and recent studies are so contradictory, that we will resort to violence and treat of only one gospel 'according to the Hebrews'. The ancients appreciated it. They believed, rightly or wrongly, that it had affinities with the 'Hebrew' or Aramaic Gospel of Matthew, or even that it was the original of it. In the time of Eusebius a specimen, written in square Hebrew letters, was preserved in the library at Caesarea. St Jerome saw it there and discovered another copy in the Nazarene community at Beroea near Antioch. He had a more or less complete copy made and then translated it for his personal use.

The scanty remains we possess of this gospel according to the Hebrews display a care for precise and characteristic detail, and a lively manner of narration, not without interest. Here, for example, is how it relates the story of the rich young man (Mt. 19: 16 ff.):

Another rich man said to him: Master, what good thing can I do so as to live? He replied: Man, keep the Law and the Prophets. He answered, That is what I have done. He said to him: Go, sell all you possess, share it with the poor, and come, follow me. The rich man began to scratch his head; this did not please him. The Lord said to him: How can you say: 'I have kept the Law and the Prophets'? For it is written in the Law: 'Thou shalt love thy neighbour as thyself', and see, many of your brethren, children of Abraham, are covered with filth and dying of hunger, and your house is full of good things, and none of them goes out to those brethren. And he turned and said to Simon his disciple, who was sitting by him: Simon, son of John, it is easier for a camel to go through the eye of a needle than for a rich man to enter the kingdom of heaven.'[1]

It is vivid, perhaps too vivid. It gives the impression of being a popular style of narration, grounded on the traditional material.

The man with the withered hand (Mt. 12: 9–13) petitions Christ in these words:

I was a mason, earning a living with my hands: I pray you, Jesus, restore me my health, that I may not have the shame of begging for my food.[2]

It is still the popular touch.

A certain number of gospels were current in Egypt, all turning on the common gospel material. A short fragment discovered at Fayyum makes a synopsis of Mk. 14: 16–30 and Mt. 26: 30–34. The dialogue between Jesus and Peter is shorter and more lively than in the canonical texts, which might be a sign of authenticity, but the fact that it is a synopsis of the story is enough to deny it any claim to originality.

In 1934 the British Museum collections were enriched by some Christian papyri. The gems of the collection were two damaged leaves and a small piece of a third leaf, remains of a gospel codex, in a script which takes us back to about A.D. 130. It was published by the editors, H. J. Bell and T. C. Skeat, under the title: *The Unknown Gospel*. We give the translation of the Greek text, adding only the titles.

---

[1] Origen, *Comm. in Matt.* 15: 14 (*P.G.* XIII, col. 1295 ff.)
[2] Jerome, *Comm. in Matt.* 12: 13 (*P.L.* XXIX, col. 78)

I. *The controversy about the Scriptures.*

Fragment 1. Verso 1. (Jesus said) to the teachers of the law, '(Blame) every betrayer of the law and godless person, but not me; for if . . . how does he do it?' Turning to the rulers of the people, he spoke to them this saying: 'Search the Scriptures; for they, in which you think you have life, testify to me. Do not think that I have come to accuse you to my Father: he who accuses you is Moses, in whom you trust.' When they said: 'We know well that God has spoken to Moses, but as for you, we do not know whence you come', Jesus answered them: 'Now does your unbelief accuse you. . . .'

II. *Attempted arrest.*

Recto 5. (So that they) might draw him, and taking up stones might stone him together. 6. And (the rulers) laid hands on him to take hold of him and deliver him to the multitude; and they could not lay hold of him because his hour to be delivered had not yet come. 7. But the Lord, escaping out of their hands, departed from them.

III. *The cure of the leper.*

8. Behold, a leper came towards him and said: 'Master, Jesus, as I was travelling with the lepers and eating with them in the inn, I myself caught the leprosy: if then you are willing, I am made clean.' 9. The Lord then said to him: 'I am willing, be made clean.' And at once the leprosy left him. 10. But the Lord said to him: 'Go, show yourself to the priests.'

IV. *Question about kings.*

Fragment 2. Recto 11. . . . (coming) to him they tempted him with their questions, saying: 'Master, Jesus, we know that you have come from God; for the things that you do give testimony above all the prophets. 12. So tell us: Is it lawful for us to render to the kings what is owed to their authority? Shall we pay it or not?' 13. But Jesus, knowing their thoughts and being angry, said: 'Why do you call me Master with your mouth, but do not listen to what I say? Well did Isaias prophesy of you when he said: This people, they honour me with their lips, but their heart is far from me: in vain do they serve me (teaching) the precepts (of men). . . .'

V. *The miracle of the Jordan.*

Verso 15. . . . 'place enclosing . . . is invisibly submitted . . . his weight, unstable. . . .' 16. When they were perplexed at his strange question, (then) Jesus walked and stood up on the bank of the river Jordan and stretching out his right hand . . . and sowed (or planted) on (the river). 17. And then . . . the water which had been sown on (or calmed) . . . and . . . in their presence and produced fruit.

This last paragraph (15–17) can be taken in a quite different sense. Fr Lagrange, agreeing in general with the editors, supposes that Jesus had asked how man, placed on the earth, can hope for a great weight of glory. Then: 'They were somewhat perplexed at his strange question, and Jesus, who was walking, stopped on the bank of the river Jordan and stretching forth his right hand he filled it with earth and sowed some wheat on the earth, and then he poured running water over it. The grain pierced the earth and sprang up before them and it produced fruit, numerous (?) for joy. . . .'[3]

Many of the features of the 'unknown gospel' suggest a harmony, in the broadest sense, of the canonical Gospels. At first sight it is chiefly inspired by John. The editors are surely too confident when they take Christ's

[3] *Critique textuelle*, II, p. 644. We suggest another hypothesis in *Muséon*, vol. XLIX (1936), pp. 70–72: that Jesus worked the miracle of sowing in the river to show he was not bound by the laws of nature.

association with lepers for a mark of authentic history. The vocabulary reveals a man of some taste; his interest in controversies with the Jews, his fondness for the Gospel of John and that of Luke, might suggest an Alexandrian.

With the 'unknown gospel' we should be inclined to connect a fragment published in 1908, whose provenance is Oxyrrhyncus. Jesus was walking in the Temple, and a discussion was going on with the Pharisees about legal purifications.[4] Of the same type is a fragment of a Coptic gospel, published by C. Schmidt in his *Actus Pauli*.[5] It reports a conversation between Jesus and his Apostles on the subject of miracles. When Jesus has recalled all those he had performed, he adds: 'If you say to this mountain: "Lift thyself and be cast into the sea", without doubting, it shall happen. . . .' Then there is talk of a miracle greater than all the others, which makes Philip angry.

Another fragment of papyrus contains the conclusion of a discourse of our Lord's, similar to the Sermon on the Mount. At the end we read: 'His disciples said to him: When wilt thou show thyself to us and when shall we see thee? He said: When you will be unclothed and will not be ashamed.' The conclusion recalls the 'Gospel according to the Egyptians', of which we shall speak later.

Alexandria likewise received a 'Gospel of Peter'. Bouriant published a long fragment of it in 1892, originating from Akhmim. The Gospel of Peter was written in Syria or Egypt, about the middle of the second century. Serapion, bishop of Antioch (196–211), found it on a pastoral visitation at Rhossos in Cilicia, in the hands of a little group of Christians. These asked to be allowed to go on reading it; without misgivings, though aware it

---

[4] J. Jeremias, in *Unbekannte Jesusworte* (Zürich, 1948), pp. 37–45, attributes a high value to this gospel fragment.

[5] Leipzig, 1904; pp. 237 ff.

was apocryphal, he at first allowed it. When he learned that the Docetist heretics were misusing this book, he changed his decision.

In the fragment which has been preserved, the story begins in the middle of the Passion and continues with the Resurrection. A few lines of it are given here.[6]

The burial anticipated.

Now Joseph, the friend of Pilate and of the Lord, standing there and knowing that they were about to crucify him, came to Pilate and asked for the body of the Lord, to bury him. And Pilate sent Herod to demand his body. And Herod said: 'Brother Pilate, even if no one had asked for him, we should have buried him ourselves, since also the sabbath is about to begin; for it is written in the Law that the sun must not set on a man put to death.' And he delivered him to the people, on the eve of the unleavened bread, their feast (3–5).

The mocking.

Now they, having taken the Lord, pushed him as they ran and said: 'Let us drag along the Son of God, for he is in our power.' And they clothed him in purple and made him sit on the judgment-seat, saying: 'Judge with equity, King of Israel.' (6–7)

The Resurrection.

Now in the night when the Lord's day dawned, while the soldiers were mounting guard two by two in their turns of duty, there was a loud noise in the heavens. And they saw the heavens opened and two men, all resplendent with light, coming down thence and approaching the tomb. And that stone which had been overset on the door rolled away of itself and went back to the side. And the sepulchre was opened and the two young men went

[6] From the French translation of L. Vaganay, *L'Évangile de Pierre* (Paris, 1930)

into it. At this sight the soldiers wakened the centurion and the elders (for they too were there), keeping guard. And while they were relating what they had seen, they now saw three men coming out of the tomb, two of them supporting the other, and a cross followed them. And the head of those two reached the sky, but the head of him they led overpassed the heavens. . . . (35–40)

It is obviously apologetic and fictional in character. Vaganay, in reaction against Harnack in particular, is rightly severe on this apocryphal writing.

Nearly all the special features of the Akhmim fragment (he considers) have their *raison d'être*, as we have seen, in the most suspect interests of apologetic. In the list which we have drawn up certain details (such as Joseph's garden), which are of value only as combining the gospel texts, must of course be excepted. There remain also three very minor points where no particularly tendency can be seen: the cross erected after the crucifixion, the garments of Jesus spread out before him, and his body being washed before burial. But there too, with such an unscrupulous author, one cannot be too cautious. He has only had to transpose the customs of his circle into the story he was writing.[7]

We must conclude that the 'living voice' was extinct for this Christian of the mid-second century, who for all that would not have been sorry to produce a new one for the edification of the faithful of Syria or Egypt. But he is brought up on the gospel story, and uses it in a very free fashion, while avoiding excessive imagination. The oral catechesis survives in principle; in actual fact it is controlled by the writing.

There is nothing specifically Gnostic in the literature we have been looking at. A little Docetism, which is no

[7] *Ibid.*, p. 128

more than the understandable desire to set Christ above
the normal level of mankind; a little Encratism, an
equally understandable exaggeration of asceticism; some
popular touches, resembling in style the stories of the
synoptic tradition; an interest in the secret teaching of
Jesus; but all this should not mislead us.

The founders of the great schools of Gnosticism were
relatively modest in the matter of gospels. In their way,
they too bear witness to the strength of the common
tradition. Among the books of the Coptic library of Nag-
Hammadi, of which we shall be speaking in a moment,
we can now read the famous 'Gospel of Truth' which
was attributed to Valentinus and is certainly worthy of
him. It is a series of meditations on the mystery of Christ's
revelation: it presumes a more than common knowledge
of the gospel literature and the Pauline Epistles. Basilides
too had composed his own gospel and is said to have
commented on it. It was only, it seems, a medley of
gospel texts mixed with legends; the 'unknown gospel'
perhaps gives us an idea of what this 'Gospel of Basilides'
was like. Marcion confined himself to mutilating the
Gospel of Luke. Tatian amalgamated the four in his
beautiful harmony.

The 'Gospel according to the Egyptians' might well be
the source of a series of apocrypha belonging to the
strictly Gnostic literature, in which heretical thought is
given full rein and reliance is boldly placed on alleged
secret revelations of the Saviour. In this category Origen
placed the *Gospel according to the Egyptians*, the *Gospel
of the Twelve*, a *Gospel of St Thomas* and a *Gospel
according to Matthias*.

We can now advance with more assured step in our
knowledge of this literature, thanks to a precious find of
eleven Coptic manuscripts at Nag-Hammadi in Upper

Egypt. In particular, one of these manuscripts has preserved the *Gospel of St Thomas*. At a single stroke has
been solved the enigma of the Gospel *logia* of Oxyrrhyncus, published in 1897 and 1904 by Grenfell and
Hunt: they are simply fragments of the Greek text of
this gospel.

The entire *Gospel of St Thomas* consists of a collection
of sentences attributed to Jesus.[8] It begins thus:

> These are the secret sayings spoken by Jesus in his life-
> time and written down by Didymus Judas Thomas. He
> says: He who finds the interpretation of these words shall
> not taste death.

Then follows 113 sentences. We translate the first two:

> (1) Jesus said: Let him who seeks cease not to seek till he
> has found, and when he finds he will be troubled, and
> if he is troubled he will marvel and he will reign over the
> whole world.
>
> (2) Jesus said: If those who draw you after them say to
> you: Behold, the kingdom is in the heavens, then the
> birds of the heavens will go before you; if they say it is
> in the sea, then the fishes will go before you. But the
> Kingdom is within you and outside you. When you shall
> know yourselves, then you will be known, and you will
> understand that you are the sons of the living God; if
> you know not yourselves, then you are in poverty and
> you are poverty.

One can imagine the immense interest such a collection
of sentences would arouse in the latter half of the second
century. Their tone would not offend even the orthodox
Gnosticism of Alexandria. But we believe the author

---

[8] Cf. G. Garitte, 'Le Premier Volume de l'Édition Photographique
des Manuscrits gnostiques Coptes et l'Évangile de Thomas', in *Le Muséon*,
vol. LXX (1957), pp. 59–73. Published in an English translation, 1959,
Collins, London.

belongs to the Valentinian school, to judge particularly by some of the eight parables of the Kingdom included in his collection. This is how he tells the parable of the lost sheep:

> (106) Jesus said: The Kingdom is like a shepherd who has a hundred sheep; the one, which is the biggest, was lost; he left the ninety-nine and searched for the one till he found it; after having worked he said to the sheep: I prefer thee to the ninety-nine.

It is Valentinus' *Gospel of Truth* which enables us to understand the two phrases, 'which is the biggest', and 'after having worked', which are additional to the canonical parable of the good shepherd. The former is an allusion to Valentinus' arithmetical allegory, which attaches great importance to the hundredth unit. (They counted up to 99 on the left hand; 100—the hundredth unit—was counted on the right hand.) The second is explained by the confusion, also found in the *Gospel of Truth*, between the lost sheep and the sheep fallen into a pit, which one pulls out only by working on the sabbath.

Clement of Alexandria has preserved in his *Stromateis* a series of replies by our Lord to questions of Salome, taken from the *Gospel according to Matthias*. Their tone is most unlike him. Salome asks: 'How long will death exert its power?' He replies: 'As long as you women go on bringing yourselves forth.' Salome replies: 'Then I have done well not to bring forth.' The Lord replies: 'Eat of every herb, but not of that which has bitterness.' They continue in this strain, and Jesus states: 'I have come to destroy the works of the woman.'

This literature needs very prudent handling, continually distorted as it is by the passion for mystery and Gnosticism.

By the end of the second century and the beginning of the third, we reach the stage of completely eccentric lucubrations and uncontrolled fantasies, remote from the Tetramorph, from tradition and from the credible. There now appear those books which pretend to contain secret teachings confided by our Lord to the Apostles or other persons after his resurrection: the *Pistis Sophia,* the *Gospel of Mary,* the *Wisdom of Jesus Christ,* the *Letter of the Apostles,* the *Books of Jeu,* an *Apocrypha of John,* and so on.[9]

There is also a final series of apocryphal gospels being produced on the fringes of the canonical books, but without heretical intent, at least in the beginning. It will be abused later on, when the less credulous and more resolute attitude of the Great Church, from the beginning of the third century, has left the monopoly of apocryphal productions to the dissident sects.

A short letter of Pilate to Claudius (Tiberius), which may have been known to Tertullian, introduces the group of *Actus Pilati,* or *Gospel of Nicodemus.*

The *Proto-evangelium* of James, drawn up by a Judaeo-Christian, may well have been composed about the middle of the second century. It was highly esteemed by the Ebionites; Clement of Alexandria seems to know it, and Justin refers to traditions connected with it. It is a popular, very attractive little book. It was given the name of *Proto-evangelium* by Guillaume Portel, who procured a manuscript of it in the East, in the sixteenth century. Its tone sometimes reminds one of Luke. Joachim and Anne are very charming. The blessed Virgin is given the education of a young nun in the Temple. Mary's early years are described and her marriage, then the miraculous conception and virginal birth of the Saviour, the arrival

[9] We expect fresh surprises from the library of Nag-Hammadi.

of the Magi and the massacre of the Innocents. Several
scenes from this gospel have passed into Christian icono-
graphy, into the Golden Legend and popular devotions;
for instance, where God chooses the aged Joseph as
husband to the blessed Virgin, by the miracle of the staff,
from which a dove emerges to alight on his head.

Another gospel of the infancy, attributed to Thomas
and found in different recensions, must be pretty old. Its
real title was: *Story of the Lord's childhood, by Thomas,
an Israelite philosopher*. The miracles attributed to Jesus
are very childish: he makes little clay birds which fly
away, and so on. There are other rather shocking features.

We must stop, if we are not to go beyond the second
century. Besides, we are far indeed from the Tetramorph.

2

When we try to visualize the text of the Gospels as
preserved in the second century, we are struck by the
notable differences which certainly existed between one
copy and another. Origen is very severe on the ancient
copyists: 'Nowadays it is an evident fact', he wrote, 'that
there is much diversity between the manuscripts, either
through the negligence of some copyists, or through the
perverse audacity of others in correcting the text, or again
at the hands of those who add or omit at their pleasure,
playing the part of correctors.'[10]

The truth is that while Christians were not lacking in
respect for the gospel and the teaching of Christ, their
respect was not so much for the text as for the teaching
itself. The text is less fixed so long as it duplicates an oral
teaching (oral tradition and catechesis) which survives

[10] In Mt. 15: 14 (*P.G.* XIII, col. 1293). Cf. L. Vaganay, *Initiation
à la critique textuelle néotestamentaire* (Paris, 1934), p. 85

and is still derived from the oral tradition of the Apostles. But these remarks afford no ground for an exaggerated distrust of the great documents which bear witness to the text; these are excellent and are generally supported when checked by more ancient papyri.

One of the most interesting of the ancient manuscripts is the Codex Cantabrigiensis, or Codex Bezae (D), a parchment written in the fifth or sixth century. It first appears in the monastery of St Irenaeus at Lyons. In 1562, when the town was sacked by the Huguenots, it was carried off from the monastery and fell into the hands of Theodore of Beza, who in 1581 gave it to the University of Cambridge. There it remains and we all know its worth. A splendid photographic edition of it was made in 1899 and Rendel Harris founded a club to study it.

It is a bilingual manuscript in Greek and Latin, containing the Gospels and the Acts, written in a country where Latin was the vulgar tongue, perhaps the south of Gaul. Its Greek text has certainly come through Egypt and in the course of its history it has acquired variants which come even from Syria. It is enriched with the sort of additions which take us back to the time when the Gospel was still a living, oral voice.

At Lk. 6: 4 it has preserved a little anecdote. 'The same day, seeing one working on the sabbath day, [Jesus] said to him: Man, if thou knowest what thou doest, happy art thou: but if thou knowest not, thou art accursed and a transgressor of the law.' The saying is profound, and well worthy of Christ. Fr Lagrange, however, points out that 'the logion only makes sense after the abrogation of the Jewish law, which was not then known to all'[11]; and this prevents our seeing in it an authentic piece of tradition.

[11] *Critique textuelle*, II, p. 66

At Lk. 23: 50, after Joseph of Arimathaea has laid Jesus in the tomb, the codex adds: 'and after he had laid him, he placed over the tomb a stone which twenty men could scarcely move'. Rendel Harris here suspected a reminiscence of the *Odyssey* (9, 240 ff.).

This same codex is one of the early witnesses for the incident of the woman taken in adultery (which we read in our Vulgate in Jn. 8: 1–11) and for the canonical ending of Mark, both of which are missing in the manuscripts of the Egyptian recension (Vaticanus, Sinaiticus, etc.).

For these two passages, then, the Codex Bezae represents authentic tradition. For Mark, we may allow the possibility of an addition made by the evangelist himself, of which our manuscript, along with others and the old versions, remains as evidence. It is not impossible that John himself may have added the incident of the woman taken in adultery, in spite of the fact that it has not the usual marks of the Johannine style. But this too might be a piece of oral tradition, invested with apostolic authority and well enough known to be admitted to the written recension of the Gospel. This is not a baseless hypothesis. We know from Eusebius of Caesarea that Papias had included the episode in his *Exposition of the Lord's Sayings*. He owed it to oral tradition, in all probability through the medium of the Elders of Asia. A precious fragment of an old tradition, coming from the Apostle John, could very rightly be inserted in the Fourth Gospel.[12]

Another fifth-century codex, bought in 1906 by Canon Freer from an Arab merchant and preserved in Washington, contained the four Gospels in the order of Matthew, John, Luke, Mark. It gives us a fresh surprise in the form of an addition after Mk. 16: 14.

[12] See M.-J. Lagrange, *Évangile selon saint Jean*, p. 225

And these pleaded: 'This age of wickedness and unbelief is under the yoke of Satan, who does not permit what is under the yoke of unclean spirits to conceive the truth and the power of God; therefore reveal now thy justice', they said to Christ. And Christ made answer: 'The number of the years of Satan's power is full; and yet even other terrible things draw near. And I was delivered to death for those who have sinned, that they may return to the truth and sin no more, that they may inherit the glory of the spiritual and incorruptible justice which is in heaven. But go ye....

'This passage', remarks Fr Lagrange, from whom we have taken the substance of the translation, 'does not give a bad impression; we may believe it to be earlier than St John's Gospel, which sanctioned the idea of judgment already given (Jn. 16: 11). It is possible that we have the faint echo of authentic sayings uttered by Jesus.[13]

Gleaning thus in the field of manuscript tradition, we might possibly, in some cases, find something of worth. It strengthens our impression that the living voice was not yet quite silent when the Christians of the first two centuries were copying the Tetramorph, but also that our 'Four' have left very few grains behind them.

3

It sometimes happens that ancient ecclesiastical authors quote sayings of Jesus which do not belong to the canonical Gospels. Sometimes they have taken them from writings now lost or just beginning to be recovered: we think of the *Gospel of St Thomas*, collections of *logia*, 'teachings', etc. Sometimes they owe them to the oral tradition, which continued to flourish alongside the written Gospels. In both cases they may have preserved

[13] *Évangile selon saint Marc*, p. 468

some good grain. So let us glean again, this time in the field of primitive Christian literature.

We must set by itself the saying preserved in the Acts, and ascribed by St Paul to the Lord Jesus: 'It is more blessed to give than to receive' (Acts 20: 35).

St Paul and St Luke lived in the full stream of oral tradition. This gospel saying is 'inspired' (in the modern sense) because of its place in the book of the Acts. For the ancients *all* the words of Jesus were endued by the 'living voice' with divine life and power. Can they have ceased to be so for us, in those admittedly quite exceptional cases in which the written Gospels or other canonical books have not recorded them and we are indebted in the last resort to oral tradition? Theologically speaking, of course, and because of the element of human judgment which separates us from them, they can never have the same weight as the inspired words.

So from among those which may have some claim to be genuine, let us glean a few more of our Lord's words.[14]

He who is near me is near the fire; he who is far from me is far from the Kingdom. (Didymus, *In Ps.* 88: 8; Orig., *In Jerem.*, hom. XX, 3)

He who is weak will be saved by him who is strong. (*Const. Apost.*, 26)

My mystery is for me and for the children of my house. (Clem. Alex., *Strom.*, V, 10, 63)

Why do you marvel at the miracles? I give you a great inheritance, which the whole world does not possess. (Macarius of Egypt, *Hom.*, XII, 17)

Ask for the great things and the small shall be given you in addition; ask for the heavenly gifts and the earthly gifts shall be given you in addition. (Clem. Alex., *Strom.*, I, 24, 158; Orig., *De Orat.*, 2, 2; 14, 1)

[14] K. Preuschen, *Antilegomena* (Giessen, 1901), pp. 44 ff.

Be well-proved bankers, proving all things, holding fast what is of value. (Clem. Alex., *Strom.*, I, 28, 177)

Because of the weak I have been weak, because of the poor I have been poor, and I have thirsted for those who are thirsty. (Orig., *In Matt.*, XIII, 2)

Thou hast seen thy brother, thou has seen thy God. (Clem. Alex., *Strom.*, I, 19, 94)

Behold, I make the last things as the first. (*Barn.*, VI, 13)

Unless you make the low to be the high, and the left to be the right, you shall not enter my kingdom. (*Acta Philippi*, 34)

CHAPTER EIGHT

Christian Life under the Sign of the Gospel

THE coming of the gospel infused fresh blood into the ageing Graeco-Roman civilization. Christian life will always beat to the rhythm of Christ's teaching. This chapter will deal briefly with the influence of the gospel and the four Gospels in the first two centuries; we shall have to speak in turn of the extraordinary success of the written Gospels, of their use in instruction for Baptism and the liturgy of the Supper, and of the development of the life of union with Christ under the sign of the Good News. Then we shall see how the Gospels were drawn into the more intellectual movements which made their appearance in Christianity from the middle of the second century: the arguments of the Apologists, the refutation of Gnosticism, the commentaries, systematic theology: in this way the idea of Christ or the Word, as revealer of God, was being ever more profoundly fathomed.

I

We have remarked what lively interest was taken in the teaching of the Apostles during the 'oral' period. From the days of the apostolic community, living in intimate contact with the Apostles' teaching, down to Papias and Polycarp, with their devout attention to the survivals of this teaching, the influence of the gospel message is continuous. The appearance of the written Gospels lessens neither the interest in the message nor its influence.

No book in the second century achieved anything like the circulation of the gospel. Vaganay writes:

> The books of the New Testament are known practically everywhere from the middle of the second century. In spite of the persecutions they will be reproduced increasingly. In fact, they constitute the real spiritual treasures of the churches—not buried treasures either; they are live and popular works. They are known by heart, quoted on every subject. Men vie with each other in interpreting them. They are alive both in memory and in practice.[1]

We have to wait till the fourth century, of course, for the appearance of those splendid editions which remain to this day and can still be consulted in privileged libraries, the Vatican or the British Museum. But this fact is easily explained. It was only then that parchment replaced the fragile papyrus from which rolls and codices had formerly been made. Even so, the sands of Egypt have yielded up some fragments, sometimes very important, of editions copied in the second century.[2]

Material survivals are anyway of slight importance. The condition in which the gospel text reaches us, when the documentation becomes abundant, gives us a glimpse of a vast publishing activity, including an incessant copying of the Gospels from the second century onwards. The remarkable multiplication of variant readings, generally dating far back, is evidence of the large number of copies.

Not only were copies multiplied, but genuine recensions were very soon put in circulation, either because it was already hoped to reduce the variety of the texts or with the desire of improving them. Those of the heretics Marcion and Tatian are best known, but the Christians of the Church in Alexandria were certainly not idle in

[1] *Initiation à la critique textuelle néotestamentaire*, p. 83
[2] See especially p. 106

this field, nor those of Rome either. The movement for revision which culminated in the great recensions of the third and fourth centuries, those of Hesychius in Egypt, Lucian at Antioch and Pamphylus at Caesarea, had already been outlined long before.

In its own way too, the weird proliferation of apocryphal gospels in the second century is a proof of the extraordinary interest which was shown in the gospel story and the sayings of Jesus. Men imitated the canonical Gospels, not in order to get away from them, but to take advantage of their popularity.

The versions, too, prove how vigorous was the life of the gospel. Christianity now reached classes of the indigenous population which did not understand much Greek. Some Latin versions, the oldest of which may well have been African, appeared from the middle of the second century. In Africa, at Rome, in North Italy, in Gaul and Spain, the Gospels were read in Latin. The style of these versions showed their popular origin: it was uncouth and vigorous, often slavishly imitating the Greek.

The Syriac-speaking churches of Syria received Tatian's *Diatessaron*. It is possible that from the second century they may also have possessed some versions of the 'distinct' Gospels. A Coptic version was soon in the hands of the Christians of Egypt; the order in which the Gospels appear in it (John, Matthew, Mark, Luke) is evidence of its antiquity.

The early Christians, then, the educated as well as the common people, read their Gospel and read it in order to know it and live by it. Far from leaving them unread in their book chests, they carried their precious manuscripts with them into their prisons. In the year 180, the proconsul Vigellius Saturninus was interrogating the martyrs Speratus, Nartzalus, Gittinus, Donata, Secunda and

Vestia, who had been arrested in the little town of Scilli. They had been convicted of the crime of being Christians. We still have the report of the proconsular Acts:

> *Saturninus the proconsul:* You can earn the pardon of our Lord the Emperor, if you will return to sound opinions.
> *Speratus:* We have never done wrong, we have not contrived any injustice, we have never slandered anyone, but when we have been maligned, we have given thanks. In this we honour our Emperor.
> *Saturninus:* What have you got in your box?
> *Speratus:* Books, and letters of Paul, a just man.

These 'books' are certainly rolls of the Gospels. Christians had themselves buried with their New Testament manuscripts, to which custom we owe certain discoveries of papyri.

2

The gospel was the main foundation for the formation of Christian morals and for teaching. That is why the Gospel of Matthew was at first held to be of greater importance than the others; the strong preference shown for it responds to these Christians' need to conform their lives to the Master's teaching.

The Sermon on the Mount provides the material for the catechizing in preparation for Baptism. The *Didache* has preserved the type of moral instruction which was given to catechumens: the influence of the Sermon is predominant.

> There are two ways: the one is of life, the other of death; but there is a great difference between the two.
> Now, the way of life is this: 'First, thou shalt love God who created thee, and secondly thy neighbour as thyself;

and do not to another what thou wouldst not have done
to thyself.'

That is precisely how Christ, in St Matthew's Gospel,
summed up the Law and the prophets and expounded the
great Christian commandment (Mt. 22: 34–40). Then
follows, in the *Didache*, the explanation of the fundamental precept, the love of our neighbour.

And this is the teaching meant by these words: Bless those
who curse you, pray for your enemies, fast for those who
persecute you. After all, what merit is there in loving
those who love you? Do the heathen not do as much?
But you must love those who hate you, and you will have
no enemy. . . . If someone gives you a blow on the right
cheek, offer him the other too, and you will be perfect;
if someone requires you to go a mile, go two miles with
him; if someone takes your cloak from you, give him your
tunic too; if anyone has taken away your goods, do not
demand them back, for you have no power to do so. Give
to whoever asks from you, asking nothing back. . . .
Happy is the man who gives, according to the commandment, for he is without blame; woe to the man who
receives; if his need obliges him to take, he is innocent.
But if he is not in need, he must answer for his motive
and object in taking; he will be put in prison and
examined on his conduct, and he will not come out of
there till he has paid the last farthing. . . .
This is the second commandment of the teaching:
'Thou shalt not kill, thou shalt not commit adultery. . . .'[3]

In order to explain the love of God and our neighbour,
the catechist draws first on the Sermon on the Mount,
then on the conversation with the rich young man
(Mt. 19: 16–21); we could not say that he merely repro-
duces the first Gospel. His great freedom as regards the
text, his additions, the allusion—'Happy is the man who

[3] *Did.*, 1, 1–2, 1

gives . . . woe to the man who receives'—to our Lord's
saying preserved in the Acts, all lead us to believe that he
is still in the main stream of oral tradition.

It is possible that the catechist of the *Didache* makes
use in his book of an ancient Jewish catechism used in
the instruction of proselytes. But it would be wrong to
speak, as A. Puech does, of 'a rather thin Christian
veneer', for it is the commandments of the Lord that set
the tone for the whole passage, and it is entirely concerned with the Lord's teaching and the Christian life.
'My son, be mindful day and night of him who teaches
you the word of God; honour him as the Lord, for where
the kingdom of the Lord is preached, there is the Lord.'
(4, 1.)

We know how the gospel was used in the Liturgy. Just
as it trained the candidates for Baptism, so for the divine
service on Sunday it provided the edifying reading which
prepared all hearts for the sacred mystery. It was chiefly
by means of the gospel, read and expounded, that Christ
was present in the assembled community, revealing to it
the secrets of God. St Justin gives a moving description
of the Sunday gathering:

On the day which is called the Sun's Day all who live in
the towns or the country meet in one place, and the
Memoirs of the Apostles or the writings of the prophets
are read, as much as time permits. When the reader has
finished, the president says some words of admonition and
exhorts us to imitate these excellent examples.

Then we all rise together, and send up our prayers to
heaven, and as I said before, when the prayer is over
the bread and wine and water are brought round; on his
part, the president offers up prayers and thanksgivings
with all his might and the people give their assent to them
by saying: *Amen*. Then takes place the distribution of

the offerings over which the thanksgiving has been pro-
nounced; each receives his share and they are sent to the
absent by the deacons. . . .[4]

The sobriety of this description almost certainly corresponds to a similar simplicity in the Roman liturgy. The
honours accorded to the Gospels in divine service cannot
go back so far, at least at Rome. In the time of St Gregory
the Great the assistants still only kiss the sacred book. In
the same period the Eastern liturgy was much more
expressive. In a letter written in 406, St Jerome notes that
throughout the East it is the custom to light candles as
a mark of joy when the Gospel is read, even by day. The
custom of placing the gospel-book on the altar (which
must be used only to hold the Body of Christ) is attested
from the middle of the third century and may be even
older. This reminds us of the phrase of St Ignatius of
Antioch, identifying the gospel with the Body of Christ.

This living contact with the Word and the life of Jesus
Christ in the gospel inspires Christians with the sense of
their profound union with Christ. St Ignatius of Antioch
reverences the gospel as the Body of Christ,[5] the perfection of eternal life.[6] He finds in it the presence of our
Saviour, Jesus Christ our Lord, his passion and his
resurrection.[7] The gospel teaches him to live as a true
disciple of Jesus Christ, the sole teacher,[8] and to imitate
him to the point of martyrdom: 'Then shall I be truly
a disciple of Jesus Christ when the world shall not even
see my body.'[9] For St Ignatius, life in Christ is governed
by the gospel.

The *Epistle of Barnabas* explains how it is that God

---

[4] *Apol.*, I, 67

[5] *Philad.*, 5, 1. To Ignatius, the word 'gospel' means the doctrine of
Christ.   [6] *Philad.*, 9, 2

[7] *Ibid.*   [8] *Magn.*, 9, 1   [9] *Rom.*, 4, 2

dwells in our souls, or in our inner temple. In us dwells 'his Word, object of our faith, the call of his promise, the wisdom of his wishes, the precepts of his teaching'.[10] It is the gospel which is envisaged.

An anonymous writing, probably to be ascribed to the end of the second century, chants the Church's hymn of exultation. The Word performs his work in souls and in the Church, and the foundation of this work is his teaching which we possess in the Gospels:

> What I have received I hand on faithfully to those who become disciples of the truth, for really now, who would not wish, once he has been rightly instructed and has come to love the Word, to strive to learn exactly what the Word taught directly to his disciples? . . . The Father sent the Word that he might show himself to the world: the Word was scorned by the [Jewish] people, preached by the Apostles, believed by the Gentiles. He is from the beginning; he appeared new and was found to be old; he is ever young, for he is born again in the hearts of the saints. Being Eternal, he today receives the name of Son. By him the Church is enriched; grace unfolds and is multiplied in the saints; grace brings understanding, reveals mysteries, announces the seasons, is rejuvenated because of the faithful: the grace of the prophets is known, the faith of the Gospels is established, the tradition of the Apostles is preserved and the grace of the Church exults.[11]

3

The Apologists, especially St Justin, stand by the traditional concept of the Gospel. Christ is 'our Teacher', the teacher *par excellence*. The most successful part of

[10] *Barn.*, 16, 9

[11] *Epistle to Diognetus*, 11, 2-6; cf. G. Bardy, *La Théologie de l'Église de saint Clément de Rome à saint Irénée*, p. 100

the doctrinal exposition of the *Apology* is that in which Justin accumulates quotations from the Gospels to prove the excellence of Christian morality. His text refers mainly to Matthew (chiefly to the Sermon on the Mount) and often also to Luke. When he has to prove that Jesus is the Son of God, it is to the 'Memoirs of the Apostles' that he has recourse,[12] as well as to the prophetic books. Never suppose that he ranks the prophets above the gospel. The importance attached by the apologist Fathers to the predictions of the prophets is explained by the needs of their argument. They are demonstrating the superiority of Christianity to the philosophies. These have no more warrant than their antiquity and the religious aura associated with the ancient philosophers, Plato in particular. Since the prophets are more ancient than Plato, the privilege of antiquity tells in favour of the Christians. But it must not be forgotten that the prophets did no more than foretell that which Christ and his Apostles taught and that it was Christ, the Word of God, who even then gave them authority and put the truth on their lips. Was it not he, too, the divine Logos, who sowed some truths in the teaching of the ancient philosophers?

The Gospel is always therefore at the heart of the Apologists' thought, foretold by the prophets, promulgated by the Apostles; it is *the* teaching above all others, for it is the explicit and perfect thought of God.

The Gospel plays an essential part in the Church's struggle against Gnosticism. The Gnostics could not escape from its dominance. So declares Irenaeus, an excellent judge: 'Such is the authority of the Gospels that the heretics themselves bear witness to them, and on them as a basis each one tries to establish his teaching.'[13]

[12] *Dial.*, 100   [13] *Adv. Haer.*, III, 11, 7

The position which the Gnostics had adopted towards the Old Testament, allowing it only a very low religious value, forced them in fact to have recourse to the New Testament and especially to the Gospels, if they were to claim to be Christians at all. Nor did they fail to do so. In this sense, they bear witness in their own way to the supreme authority exercised by the Gospels in the second century.

> Thus [concludes Irenaeus] they strengthen our position and enable us to refute them by relying on the obvious principles of the Gospels: that there is but one God, the maker of this universe, who was proclaimed by the prophets and through Moses established the dispensation of the Law, the Father of our Lord Jesus Christ, and that there is no other God, no other father.

Strong in the evidence which flows from the Gospel, the Church will for ever maintain the unity of God and the continuity of the Old Testament with the New, in the unity of one single revelation.

It is no mere accident that the first 'commentary' on the Gospels, that of Heracleon on John, saw the light in Alexandria, and in the school of Valentinus. It is moreover a remarkable work in more than one respect.

The literal explanation of the text is often perfectly accurate. The allegorical aspect is restrained. But it is here, none the less, that the shoe pinches.

Any commentary on St John, in the modern sense of the word, must be allegorical, in the sense that it must bring out the allegorical meaning which the author had in mind, over and above the surface meaning of the words. The allegorical sense, to our minds, is still the literal sense, since it is that which the author had in view.

Heracleon is not always bound by this scruple; he often substitutes his own imaginings for John's allegorical allusions.

His commentary on the Samaritan woman is a very successful effort of its type. The woman is the symbol of the soul in search of God, meeting the Saviour. It is soberly conceived and very effective. The same cannot be said of his commentary on the 'little king' of Caphar-naum. This 'little king', the *regulus* of our Vulgate, represents the Demiurge, but this is clearly contrary to the idea of the Gospel. Heracleon resorts to allegory in order to insinuate his own theories into the text.

It seemed perfectly natural, in Alexandria, to write an 'allegorical' commentary; any other would have been inconceivable. Philo had made this sort of interpretation fashionable for the Old Testament, and before that there had been the allegories by which the philosophers explained mythology.

The masters of the Christian Didascalia at Alexandria, Pantaenus, Clement and Origin, lived in this intellectual milieu and breathed its air. We no longer possess the book of *Hypotyposes*, in which Clement made an abridged commentary on the whole of Scripture, by explaining detached phrases. They were only rough drafts. The first Catholic commentator was Origen.

Grammarian, philologist, historian, theologian and mystic, this genius is the creator of the Catholic com-mentary and the homily. He wrote commentaries on the Gospels of Matthew, Luke and John: he preached homi-lies on Matthew and Luke. He carefully explains the literal meaning, often with a true master's touch.[14] This done, he erects a scaffolding of higher meanings on the

---

[14] Cf. H. de Lubac, in *Origène*, 'Homélies sur la Génèse' (*Sources chrétiennes*) (Paris, 1943), pp. 40–55

base of the literal. Once again, this principle cannot be ruled out, especially with St John. But it all depends on how it is done and we cannot but agree with A. Puech, that 'the personal views developed by Origen . . . are usually in themselves very rich in substance and most deserving of our interest; they do not constitute that strict exegesis we have a right to expect.'[15]

Thus at Alexandria, in the second half of the second century, appeared the type of gospel commentary which had such a great future before it. (We cannot really describe Papias' *Exposition of the Lord's Sayings* as a commentary. With the contents of the canonical Gospels Papias mixed traditions taken down from the lips of the Elders and his own reflections, which often have little connexion with the text to which they refer.)

In the process of expounding the main lines of the gospel message to the pagans and insisting on its monotheistic teaching, on its pure, austere morality which responds to the highest aspirations of man's reason, the Apologists raised Christianity to the level of what the ancients called a philosophy. It is a philosophy revealed by the Word of God: we more rightly call this teaching a theology. Theology is based from the outset on the Gospel. The alliance between Christianity and religious philosophy, even a kind of theosophy, was sealed at Alexandria in a more original fashion. From now on some thinkers search the Christian scriptures, and especially St John, for divine revelations, which they expect to illuminate their intellects by *gnosis*: when the letter of the Gospels does not seem to them profound enough, they apply to them the methods inherited from the pagan mysteries or from Platonism and Stoicism.

The movement degenerated into heresy from the start,

[15] *Histoire de la littérature grecque chrétienne*, II, p. 386

with Valentinus, Basilides and their disciples. They developed two theses which clash with the true meaning of the gospel message: first, that the Old Testament was the work of a secondary god, inferior or even bad, and second, that Christian 'gnostics' formed a natural aristocracy within Christianity, enjoying a separate régime in this world and the next. The Christian doctors of the Church, Irenaeus and Hippolytus, and Justin before them, relying firmly on the apostolic tradition preserved in the churches founded by the Apostles and on the canonical Gospels, demonstrated that the Gnostic theses belong less to Christianity than to camouflaged paganism, and they were overwhelmingly justified.

The Christian teachers of the Didascalia at Alexandria, however, did their best to confine the conflagration, and abandoning theories which were really heretical, they searched the Christian revelation for that wisdom superior to Greek philosophy, which St Paul had already called the Christian wisdom 'in a mystery'.

Stimulated by this movement of orthodox Gnosticism in Alexandria, the Apologists had then to reflect on the meaning of the Christian revelation, which could henceforth compete with Greek philosophy in its own sphere, and on the character of Christ as the revealer. The 'moral teacher' of the Sermon on the Mount was the Son of God: he was Son, because he was the Speech of God coming forth from silence, the Word, the Logos. Theology began to explore the data of the gospel; the Church began to take possession of her spiritual riches, born of the revelation of the Word of God. At last she had the glorious chance of showing the Greek world that this Master who, in the gospel, 'taught with authority' and captivated men's souls, who 'had the words of eternal life', who was the Logos of God, Life, Light and Truth, was in fact *the final word which God had spoken to all men*, and that souls would henceforth hear in him the only music able both to charm them and to assure their salvation.

The new song of the Word of God—that is what the gospel is. And so in the beginning of his *Protrepticus*, Clement, in 'his love for mankind', invites it to go to school with the Word. The pagan legends have had their day, Amphion of Thebes who charmed the fishes, Orpheus who tamed wild beasts. . . .

> Again I could recite to you a sister-legend to these, tell you another singer, Eunomus the Locrian, and the grasshopper of Delphi. The Greeks were assembled at Delphi to celebrate the death of the dragon, while Eunomus was chanting the reptile's epitaph: the serpent's praise or his dirge? I cannot say. But there they were all assembled, and Eunomus was playing at the hour of the dogstar. Behind the leaves, on the hills, the grasshoppers were singing, burning in the sunlight. They were singing, you may be sure, not for the slaughtered dragon of Pytho, but for the most wise god, and singing in their own mode, far better than the tunes of Eunomus. One of the Locrian's strings breaks; the grasshopper leaps on to the neck of the lute and trills on the instrument as on a branch; so following her song, the musician continues to play on the remaining string. But it is not the singing of Eunomus which prompts the grasshopper, as the legend has it which has caused bronze statues of Eunomus and his singing partner to be set up at Delphi; no, the grasshopper springs of her own accord and sings in her own fashion. But in the eyes of the Greeks she appears as having interpreted his music.

Henceforth there is but one singer, the 'heavenly Logos, the true athlete, crowned on the stage of the whole world'.

He sings, this Eunomus of mine, not in the mode of
Terpander nor of Capio, still less in Phrygian, Lydian or
Dorian mode, but in the mode of the new harmony, the
mode which bears the name of God: he sings the new
song of the Levites, endowed with a charm 'which
banishes grief and calms wrath, which brings oblivion of
all woes' [Homer, *Odyssey*, IV, 221], sweet and perfect
remedy for pain. . . .

No sooner has he come than he hastens to overthrow
the bitter slavery imposed by the tyranny of the demons,
and, placing us under the easy and humane yoke of goodness [Mt. 11: 30], he calls back to heaven those who had
been cast down to earth. He it is, in truth, who alone has
tamed the fiercest animals ever known, I mean men:
birds, like the frivolous; serpents, like deceivers; lions,
like the violent; swine, like sensualists; wolves, like
robbers. Stone and wood are without sense, but more
senseless than stone is man, plunged in error! Let our
witness be the voice of the prophets, which, being in tune
with the voice of truth, groans over those who live in
ignorance and folly: 'God can raise up children of Abraham from these stones' [Mt. 3: 9]—God, who in his pity
for the great ignorance and hard-heartedness of those
who have become as stone towards the truth, has raised
up a new stock of religion, apt for virtue, from among
those petrified nations which have put their faith in
stones. Moreover the voice of Truth has branded as a
'brood of vipers' certain malicious men, crafty hypocrites,
who barred the way to justice; and yet if any one of
these serpents really intends to come to repentance, he
becomes, by following the Logos, 'a man of God'. Others
God describes as 'wolves in sheep's clothing' (Mt. 7: 15),
meaning those who under the forms of men are ravening
wolves. Now all these, who are the fiercest beasts and as
it were stones, by the heavenly song have been turned into
civilized men. . . .

The Logos of God, scorning those soulless instruments

the lyre and the lute, through the Holy Spirit mastered the world, and in particular man, this microcosm, his body and his soul; he makes use of this polyphonic instrument to praise God, and himself sings in tune with this human instrument. . . .

The Logos of God, the Lord—what would he then with this instrument and his new song? What but to open the eyes of the blind and the ears of the deaf, to guide the lame and the strayed to justice, to reveal God to senseless men, to put an end to corruption, to vanquish death, to reconcile the disobedient children to the Father? He loves mankind, that instrument of God: he instructs, exhorts, warns, saves and protects us, and in reward for our obedience he promises us, in addition, the Kingdom of Heaven, not willing to accept from us any advantage save one, our own salvation. Evil feasts on men's loss, but the truth, like the bee which soils nothing on earth, rejoices only in their salvation. Here then in your hands is that object of the promise, here is this love for men! Accept your share in that grace. And for this saving song of mine, do not think its newness is that of some furnishing or of a house, for 'I was before the dayspring', and 'in the beginning was the Word, and the Word was with God, and the Word was God' [John 1 : 1].[16]

[16] *Protrepticus*, I, 1–6

Reflection

FROM the Master of the Sermon on the Mount to the 'heavenly Logos', singing on 'the stage of the whole world', is not such a long journey as might appear. The narrow stage of the Galilaean hills was capable of infinite enlargement, for there the voice of the ultimate prophet spoke to all mankind and for ever.

The Apostles stood closer to Jesus than others. The words of life were graven on their memories, the vivid memories of simple men, and the Holy Spirit filled them with his power; thus these words became the apostolic message. The first two or three generations of Christians enjoyed the privilege of living by the 'oral' message.

The living voice, if it is to be 'permanent', must normally resort to writing. God did not dispense the apostolic message from this general necessity. The Apostle Matthew was the first to put the oral tradition into writing: Mark followed him, using Peter's catechesis as his basis. Luke, Paul's disciple and as enterprising as his master, wrote a book for the educated. The aged Apostle John, surrounded by his Asian Christians and conscious of being 'the disciple whom Jesus loved', was entitled to penetrate further into the secrets of the Word, who had been sent unto his own, and his own had received him not. Christians of the future would have no cause to envy the earliest.

Even so, the second-century generations felt the yearning for the 'living voice'. Papias, Polycarp and Irenaeus are in full sympathy with it. But the Gnostics, for less worthy ends, corrupted a harmless tendency, just when the fantastic 'apocrypha' were being let loose. They were too late. The four written Gospels had fixed the message for good. A few handfuls of corn, among so much cockle, are of little import beside the overflowing waggonloads of good ripe sheaves.

Christian theology reaped the harvest. It made from them the foursquare stack, solidly based on the 'tetra-morphic gospel'. The Apologists worked on it, and all those, like Irenaeus, who ensured the firmness of the Christian faith against fantasy and the spirit of heresy. Bolder still, Clement of Alexandria and Origen could henceforth invite the Greeks, with their passion for music and philosophy, to the harvest feast.

'The living and permanent voice'; such is the gospel message, such are our four inspired Gospels. In them the voice of the Word of God goes on, witness and life, life and witness, inseparably united. Because it is a living voice, it is still *spoken* today by a living person: the Church, in whom, through her princes, the successors of the Apostles, and through her members, the Word of God continues his life in time.